IN-BETWEEN BODIES

SUNY SERIES IN GENDER THEORY
Tina Chanter, editor

IN-BETWEEN BODIES

Sexual Difference, Race,
and Sexuality

MARY K. BLOODSWORTH-LUGO

STATE UNIVERSITY OF NEW YORK PRESS

Cover art: *Ambiguity* by Amanda L. Murray

Published by
STATE UNIVERSITY OF NEW YORK PRESS, ALBANY

© 2007 State University of New York

All rights reserved

Printed in the United States of America

For information, contact State University of New York Press, Albany, NY
www.sunypress.edu

Production, Laurie Searl
Marketing, Anne M. Valentine

Library of Congress Cataloging-in-Publication Data

Bloodsworth-Lugo, Mary K.
  In-between bodies : sexual difference, race, and sexuality / Mary K. Bloodsworth-Lugo.
     p. cm. — (SUNY series in gender theory)
  Includes bibliographical references and index.
  ISBN 978-0-7914-7221-7 (hardcover : alk. paper)
  ISBN 978-0-7914-7222-4 (pbk. : alk. paper)
  1. Sex differences. 2. Sex role. 3. Race—Sex differences. I. Title.

HQ1075.B58 2007
306.7—dc22   2007002076

10 9 8 7 6 5 4 3 2 1

For Carmen

Te amo con todo mi corazón . . . por siempre.

CONTENTS

ACKNOWLEDGMENTS

I would like to thank the philosophy departments of The University of Memphis and Washington State University for their support during different stages of this project. In particular, I would like to thank Tina Chanter (DePaul University) for her constructive feedback on my work and friendship over the years. I would like to thank my colleagues in the women's studies department at Washington State University for their support during my time there. I would also like to thank Jane Bunker, at SUNY press, for her encouragement during the development of this project, and the two anonymous SUNY readers for their helpful remarks on improving the manuscript.

I would like to acknowledge my undergraduate students at Washington State University, especially those in my sections of Lesbian and Gay Studies, Women and Ethics, Philosophy and Feminism, and the Lesbian and Gay Studies Reading Group for their kindness in engaging with my ideas over the years. I would like to thank the graduate students in my American studies seminars for providing productive sites for discussion. I would also like to thank my former philosophy student Kasey Gorman for proofreading a nearly completed copy of the manuscript, and I would like to acknowledge women's studies alum Amanda L. Murray for creating and providing the book's cover art titled, "Ambiguity."

I would like to thank my colleague, Kendal L. Broad, at the University of Florida, for co-authoring a paper that became chapter 5 of this book. Earlier versions of several chapters of the book were first presented as conference papers: Chapter 6 was presented under the title "Sexual Difference Theories and Same-Sex Couples: Is Sexual Difference Theory Heterosexist?" at the Pacific American Philosophical Association (APA) Meeting in Seattle, Washington, 2002; chapter 5 was presented as "Teaching Lesbian and Gay Studies" at the Thirty-Ninth Annual Meeting of the Society of Phenomenology and Existential Philosophy (SPEP) in State College, Pennsylvania, 2000; chapter 4 was presented as "Gender Transgression and Sexual Difference" at the Thirty-Eighth Annual Meeting of SPEP in Eugene, Oregon, 1999; chapter 2 was presented as "Irigaray's (Re-)Figuring of Place: Sexual Difference, Ambiguity, and Aristotle's *Physics* IV" at the Thirty-Seventh Annual Meeting of SPEP in Denver, Colorado, 1998; components of chapters 1 and 3 were published as "Embodiment and Ambiguity: Luce Irigaray,

Sexual Difference, and 'Race,' " in *International Studies in Philosophy* (31, no. 2 [1999]: 69–90).

More personally, I would like to recognize my partner, Carmen, for her daily presence in my life and reminder of how wonderful it can be. *Tú eres el amor de mi vida*. I would also like to thank her/our family—Carmen, Kermit, Kermit, Madeline, and Alvin—for welcoming me into their lives. Finally, I would like to thank my father, Walter, for providing me with many years of support. My mother, Elaine, and my brother, Randy, did not live to see many things, but they remain in my thoughts and inform my choices daily.

RETHINKING BODIES

An argument could be made that the beloved category of "gender," so commonly used in feminist theory to avoid the problems of essentialism, could be understood not as the attribution of social and psychological categories to a biologically given sex but in terms that link gender much more closely to the specificities of sex.

—Grosz 1994

[She is] somewhere between monster and mammy: demanding, demeaning, impossible to please, but at the same time possessing irresistible custodial power and erotic allure as the larger than life (racialized) Other.

—duCille 1996

Feminist theories of sexual difference have garnered significant recent focus. Theorists such as Rosi Braidotti (1994), Judith Butler (1993, 1990), Rosalyn Diprose (1994), Moira Gatens (1996, 1991), Elizabeth Grosz (1994), and Luce Irigaray (1993, 1985) have articulated conceptions of sexual difference, and in so doing, these theorists have reconfigured "the body." If bodies are rendered as subject to interpretation, as these scholars suggest, rather than as given, static, neutral things, then the traditional relation between subject and object, and between mind and body—as well as our very formulations of identity and subjectivity—are recast. Characteristic of sexual difference frameworks is their construal of bodies as both produced by and resistant to production by social, historical, and cultural practices. Bodies, that is, are rendered as ambiguous between construction and constraint.

Importantly, sexual difference theorists have aimed to uncover bodies from their neglected status within the histories of both (Western) philosophy and (egalitarian) feminism. Western philosophy has traditionally ignored "the body" since philosophy has been thought to reside in "the mind," and

1

egalitarian feminism has downplayed bodies because a focus on women's bodily differences has been feared as upholding women's inferior status in relation to men. By rethinking bodies, sexual difference theorists have rethought the issue of (sexual) difference in nonessential ways. Rather than being considered given and natural objects, bodies have been conceived as produced by social/cultural/historical influences while being resistant to those very processes of production.

In the present work, I highlight sexual difference theories as offering powerful frameworks for rethinking issues of sex and gender, identity, and subjectivity. I argue that the analyses offered by sexual difference theories, while focused on the difference between the sexes, may be productively applied to matters of race and ethnicity, transgender experience, classroom pedagogy, and queer politics. I maintain that recent efforts to rethink "the body" have effectively posited bodies as residing in-between classically conceived oppositional categories. Likewise, events unfolding in-between bodies (for example, the binaries of male/female bodies and white/black bodies) have proven to be significant sites of theoretical investigation. I claim that the in-between position afforded and analyzed by sexual difference theories, as well as by recent theories of race and sexuality, offers a means to conceptually adjudicate between traditionally opposing terms. Within these accounts, bodies are reconfigured to reveal identities as both subject to constraint and open to radically different configurations. While I examine and maintain the practical extension of sexual difference theories beyond a consideration of sex and gender, I also uncover and question their potential limits.

Making links between sexual difference, race, and sexuality, apart from being a productive project in itself, serves to address charges sometimes made against sexual difference theories and other analyses of "the body." For example, some writers have maintained that sexual difference theories precisely neglect racial and other forms of difference—thereby advancing an implicitly *white* notion of sexual difference (cf. Butler 1993). In addition, some scholars have claimed that despite their purported focus on the body, body theories are often "strangely disembodied" (cf. Davis 1997). Cecilia Sjöholm has pointed out that "The strange thing about Irigaray's texts is that . . . she says surprisingly little about the female body. . . . There is not much body, nothing to be seen. In her elemental writings, there is no matter at all" (2000, 97). While I agree with these claims, I engage such critiques by arguing that sexual difference frameworks have significant practical import—import not always articulated by the theories and theorists themselves. I offer a series of concrete examples to demonstrate how sexual difference theories could be more broadly instantiated (even if the theoretical work itself is often lacking such examples). Although sexual difference theories may—ironically at times—lack a materiality characteristic of the lived bodies that they advance, I suggest ways that sexual difference theories could nonetheless find constructive application.

One instance of this application is to note that recent claims regarding bodies can be maintained as holding not only for sexually marked bodies, but also for "raced" or racialized bodies. The negative meaning that has been attributed to "blackness" or "darkness" can be traced to specific conceptions of the (black/dark) body. While women's bodies have been conceived as atrophied versions of men's, black bodies have been viewed as overdeveloped variations of white, European ones. Consequently, notions of both underdevelopment and overdevelopment of bodies have been used to conclude sexual and racial inferiority.

Regarding charges that feminist bodily theorizing is often strangely *dis*embodied, it can be said that given the centrality of a notion of the *lived* body within sexual difference analyses, the body as lived—by definition—is not a detached body. "Positioned" in-between the biological (body) and the cultural (society), lived bodies transcend mere biology. At the same time, lived bodies do not float off into disembodied space; that is, away from ordinary, corporeal, and everyday experiences. Thus, sexual difference theories have the virtue of both loosening the constraints or limitations on bodies (and the relation between sex and gender) and positing the conditions for these very restrictions in the first place. In this way, lived bodies can be considered to be exemplary in-between bodies.

As mentioned above, sexual difference reappraisals of bodies have likewise fostered reformulations of Western notions of identity and subjectivity. Within sexual difference accounts, subjectivities do not reside "in" minds; rather, subjects are (re-)located as embodied. More precisely, subjectivity is situated in the space in-between mind (culture) and body (nature). To say that bodies are theorized as always lived is to say that they never exist independent of social, historical, and cultural contexts. If bodies are shown to "bleed" their traditionally relegated borders and boundaries, then Western formulations of identity also exceed containment. As Anne Caldwell has indicated, "If fluid elements are remembered, as Irigaray suggests, matter appears not as inert but as porous and capable of materialization. In such a fluid economy of intervals, material relationships whose terms can never be fully separated structure concepts and subjectivity" (2002, 24). And as Sjöholm has claimed, with respect to Irigaray and Merleau-Ponty's notion of the *chiasm*, "Bodies do not melt into one another . . . the excess of the feminine becomes, if you like, the guardian of an open space. And yet that space is continuously threatened" (2000, 106).

An example of the fact that this "open space" is both perceived as a threat and itself threatened can be found in transgendered experience. To identify or to be perceived as transgendered is to embody a "violation" of static conceptions of identity; it is to visibly defy the strict and policed borders of normalcy. Importantly, sexual difference theories highlight the possibility that if bodies—all bodies—always exceed "their own boundaries" (as Butler specifically states), and if bodies are never static and polarized (despite Western ideas and desires to the contrary), then transgendered bodies/ subjects make this persistent disruption evident. Trans-bodies transgress and threaten dichotomous/dualistic borders, revealing many presumed polarities as never quite polar. Trans-bodies vividly indicate that identity itself is always already a matter of bleeding and extension, and they do so in a unique way vis-à-vis the theoretical distinction between sex and gender.

A reconception of the relationship between sex and gender is precisely central to the recent reconfiguration of bodies. Gatens (1991), for instance, has articulated a relation of "contingency" between the categories of sex and gender—arguing that the sex/gender relationship is neither necessary nor arbitrary. That is to say, femininity does not have to attach to the female body at all (nor masculinity to the male body). Nonetheless, the tendency for particular sex/gender mappings to occur is not purely arbitrary, since, for one thing, socially expected mappings are rewarded and unexpected gender assumptions are punished. Thus, Butler (1993) has argued for the normative nature of the category *sex*. "Sex" is not simply a natural classification at all; instead, "sex" is constituted by and operates under certain social pressures and controls.

The present project participates in efforts to reconceive sex and gender by expanding upon Gatens's notion of contingency. To view a relation as contingent means to see the terms involved as neither fixed, on the one hand, nor unconnected, on the other hand. Rather than serving to "fix" the subject, an emphasis on the in-between posits and maintains the dynamic "nature" of the body-subject. Thus, the idea of a contingent relation between terms may be stretched beyond rethinking sex and gender. Instead, it can serve to guide the reformulation of many classically conceived categories of opposition. Sexual difference theories have focused on what lies in-between standard terms of opposition and have posited a middle position often ignored or rendered invisible by and within traditional frameworks. To emphasize the *in-between* is also to keep with Caldwell's reading of Irigaray in that Caldwell remarks, "By recovering the forgotten passage connecting the material and the intelligible, Irigaray shows that concepts and subjectivity emerge within a dynamic interaction between the material and the intelligible. . . . A sensible transcendental, participating in both the material and the ideal, disarrays the traditional oppositions between these domains" (2002, 24). And, as Caldwell continues, "Insofar as material mediation does not require the exclusion of materiality and ambiguity, a fluid economy creates the possibility of a community capable of recognizing, rather than excluding, difference" (25).

As an example of how a contingent sex/gender relation can be used as a model for addressing "other" relationships, we can discuss the connection between "raced bodies" and "raced cultures." That is to say, different meanings have been attributed to "whiteness" mapped onto "black bodies" and "whiteness" attached to "white bodies," and vice versa. This fact undermines efforts to define race simply in terms of skin color, since different significances emerge from connections between "raced" characteristics and particularly "colored" bodies. The fact that these relations do indeed differ, and that they have weight, is evident in the cases of "passing" and tanning. Hence, it is the relationship between body and color that is the bearer of meaning.

Like all Western dualistic structures, "the races" have been defined according to a logic of mutual exclusion. Hence, to be outside of purport-edly divided and contained racial categories is to have no place—it is to lack (or defy) definition. Another way to make this point is to say that despite the liberating and resistant potential of in-between positions, to exist in-between extremes has nonetheless been difficult for individuals so "situated." This means that living one's body within a traditionally unrec-ognized and invisible region is to reside in a space not easily tolerated by prescribed boundaries of demarcation. Furthermore, the meanings attrib-uted to certain bodies vary depending on their associated landscape. As Radhika Mohanram indicates, describing her move from the United States to New Zealand, "In New Zealand I was referred to as 'black' whereas in the U.S. I have always been labeled 'brown' " (1999, xii). In the pages that follow, I address the issue of how "mappings" of "colors" to "bodies" varies depending upon the implications of context. Racialization processes make clear that races are neither simply given nor are they purely made. Rather, "races" are located in-between what is granted (essential) and what is adopted (constructed).

This point, that "races" are situated within contexts and structures, connects with Irigaray's consideration of sexual difference, since for Irigaray sexual difference marks an *approach*. As Irigaray states, sexual difference rep-resents "a way of thinking that's been forgotten in the West" (1993a, 6). By articulating sexual difference as an approach, to rethink bodies means to interrogate the structure of Western thinking—revealing how sexual differ-ence serves to unsettle its logic. In particular, Western binaries are reframed and undermined through a thwarting of "either . . . or" thought. Given Irigaray's approach to sexual difference, "difference" is recast in non–mutually exclusive ways. Thus, all forms of difference (that is, differences grounded in Western binary thinking) are opened to reformulation. In this regard, Gatens's notion of a contingent relation between sex and gender can be linked with Irigaray's approach to sexual difference, since Western evaluative systems have excluded in-between categories as conceivable positions of subjectivity. However, these in-between positions become more viable given a sexual difference framework. As Sjöholm states, "The body is an intersection from which our experience of the world opens up. But that intersection never unfolds in a harmonious way" (2000, 101). She continues, "Moving cross-wise, mirroring, consuming, stirring, bordering each other, the 'I' and the 'you' are engaged in a continuous process of change. The notion of difference as 'more than one' is set against sexual duality" (104–105).

Keeping with the notion of sexual difference as an approach, it can also be said that sexual difference theories could inform sexualities pedagogy. To introduce sexual difference theories into pedagogical discussions serves to complicate the relationship between sex/gender and sexuality, and between feminism and queer theory. In the present project, I maintain that "queer" perspectives on teaching Lesbian, Gay, Bisexual, Transgender, and Queer (LGBTQ) studies have come to be characterized by a pedagogical interplay between identity and anti-identity. I argue for the extension of an identity/anti-identity teaching philosophy to incorporate the bodily materiality and constructive ambiguity highlighted by sexual difference theories. I claim that a sexual difference pedagogy would be situated at the interstices in-between identity and anti-identity, standpoint and deconstruction. Thus, the pedagogical application of sexual difference theories offers a way to maintain the feminist edge to teaching queer lessons.

Finally, it is important to note that sexual difference theories have been charged with heterosexism; that is, the accusation has been made that the concept of "sexual difference" is premised on a male-female pairing that excludes female-female and male-male pairings from its purview. On the other hand, it is also significant to notice that some readers of Irigaray (in particular) have claimed to find lesbian sexuality within her texts. My proposal, here, is to support a view suggesting that given the dominance of a heterosexist lens and frame of reference, any shift in representation—including that signaled by the claim to rethink sexual difference—can readily render a "marked" category. I use the example of children's television show characters (notably, Tinky Winky from the Teletubbies) and point out that a character can easily be labeled "gay" simply in virtue of not enacting a typically invisible, but nonetheless expected, heterosexual role. By way of the Jerry Falwell incident involving Tinky Winky, I conclude that a politics of identity, informed by sexual difference theories, may be of greater practical import than the proliferation of boundaries enabled by "queer." I maintain that Falwell effectively rendered a queer reading of Tinky Winky—one perhaps more "queer" than that of "queer communities" themselves.

I examine these and related puzzles with an aim, again, of pressing sexual difference theories on the issue of what is included within and excluded by their frameworks. I provide a more sustained treatment of sexual difference theories in chapter 1 of the text, including a discussion of Gatens's notion of a contingent relation between sex and gender and its connection to Irigaray's approach to sexual difference. I emphasize how Western evaluative systems have excluded in-between categories as conceivable positions of subjectivity but how these positions become feasible through reconceptions of bodies. I then turn to the work of Luce Irigaray in chapter 2, in order to illustrate a theoretical model of ambiguity. I focus on Irigaray's figures of Diotima, the womb, and the category "woman"—all of which may be considered in-between bodies. Diotima, like love (*eros*), is intermediate between pairs of opposites. By mediating between traditionally opposing terms, Diotima—and her conception of *eros*—fosters between men and women an "innovative" relation in which *eros* is not subjected to a telos. My primary concern in this reading is to trace the two movements in the speech of Diotima. I show how the issue of sexual difference is both revealed and concealed within "her" discourse. Likewise, I examine Irigaray's reading of Aristotle's treatise on place in *Physics* IV. For Irigaray, "The transition to a new age requires a change in our perception and conception of *the inhabiting of places*" (1993a, 7). To refigure place means to rethink the interval or relation between form and matter. As Dorothea Olkowski remarks, "In calling on the interval and conceptualizing it as the moment in which all traditional metaphysical relations are transformed . . . Irigaray (or at least her readers) cannot help but recognize that relations other than those between man and woman are at stake here too and that the interval is a crucial element in transforming situated embodiment . . ." (2000, 82). I suggest that Irigaray both locates and finds absent such a rethinking of embodiment within Aristotle's own treatment of place. Much like Irigaray's writing itself, this chapter should be mostly read as performative in its treatment of ambiguity; that is, rather than delineate what ambiguity is in propositional terms, this chapter aims to provide contextualized examples of how Irigaray views ambiguity as performing and operating in the selected texts of Plato and Aristotle. While Irigaray continues to provide inspiration throughout the book—indeed, I precisely wish to return to Irigaray to demonstrate where her theoretical model fails—my concentrated focus on Irigaray's work is represented here.

I engage sexual difference theories with recent literature regarding the categories of *race* and *transgender* in chapter 3 and chapter 4. Here, my discussion is situated within recent debates in the philosophy of race/ethnicity and lesbian/gay/queer studies concerning what constitutes an African American philosophy (cf. Outlaw 1996) and what difference high queer theory makes to ordinary queer lives (cf. Feinberg 1996). As mentioned above, I examine both how sexual difference theories could productively inform articulations of race and transgender, as well as how sexual difference theories ultimately fail to capture the nuances associated with these categories. Ironically, in making this claim, I also suggest that sexual difference theories do not adequately account for the sex/gender relation either—the very relationship most central to the theories themselves. That is to say, insofar as sex and gender cannot be adequately theorized apart from their interplay with other social categories of identity (for example, race, class, and sexuality), attempts to consider sex and gender in isolation from these categories are rendered structurally and methodologically unsound. I focus on *contingency*, especially in chapter 3, in order to examine the in-between position of bodies given different meanings rendered by various mappings of bodies to social and cultural inscriptions. In chapter 4, I address how trans-bodies reveal the difficulty of living between extremes—within an unrecognized region not easily afforded by mutually exclusive categories—while they also reveal the everyday extension of bodies themselves.

I examine what a concept of the in-between might mean for pedagogy and politics in chapter 5 and chapter 6. I discuss consequences that result when the ambiguity and contingency supported throughout the book fail to be enacted—or, more accurately when ambiguity and contingency are not adequately grounded. For instance, in chapter 5, I address the downside of teaching a course such as lesbian and gay studies from the premise of sexual fluidity (demonstrated by points such as, "You never know who in your life is gay," or more strongly, "We are all a little bit gay [and/or queer])." I argue in favor of a pedagogy highlighting *in-between bodies* grounded in sexual difference theory, and I offer concrete teaching examples that focus on the materiality of bodies and that foster new understandings of identity and subjectivity in the sexualities classroom. Likewise, in chapter 6, I address the failure of many transgender people to feel liberated by an agenda of gender fluidity, preferring instead to "reify" categories most suited to them. I maintain that the concept of fluidity is open to an ironic and exclusionary implementation. Within this discussion, I also address the question of whether the concept of queer has outlived its usefulness, and I suggest that a response to this question primarily turns on considering how "queer" has been applied to an ever-expanding array of contexts. As mentioned above, I claim that a politics of identity, enabled by sexual difference theories, may have greater practical applicability than the proliferation of boundaries signaled by "queer."

Finally, a brief discussion of terminology employed in the text might be useful in guiding the reader. The overarching concept of the text, as noted above, is that of in-between bodies. This concept involves the notion that bodies are both located in the space in-between traditional categories of opposition, and that what unfolds in-between bodies themselves is open to theoretical investigation. Thus, there is a certain ambiguity to in-between bodies that may be explained as follows. In using the term *ambiguity*, I aim to signal *both . . . and* positions that are often set in opposition to classically conceived *either . . . or* formulations. As examples, we might note that one is usually considered to be *either* white *or* black, or a man *or* a woman; one is not considered capable of being *both* white *and* black, or a man *and* a woman. Sexual difference theories focus on ambiguity insofar as they highlight *both . . . and* relations. While "ambiguity" may have a range of everyday meanings, I primarily intend this *both . . . and* logic through my use of the term here.

Likewise, while the term *contingent* can mean "arbitrary" in everyday usage, I differentiate "contingent" from both "arbitrary" and "necessary" in the present project. Rather than marking a relationship between categories that is either arbitrary or necessary, a contingent relation suggests that the connection between categories/terms/bodies is neither random nor compulsory. The concept of contingency indicates that various mappings of mind to body, or gender to sex, or culture to race, do not render symmetrical meanings. As Gatens notes, masculinity mapped onto the male body is not equivalent to masculinity mapped onto the female body. Thus, sexual difference, and not gender, is of central concern in this project. For this reason, the term *sexual difference* replaces the more typical feminist designation *gender* in the subtitle. However, insofar as this book does address "gender" (apart from the use of the construct by egalitarian and degendering feminists), it is by way of trans*gender* experiences. Trans-bodies vividly demonstrate the array of difficulties posed by nonnormative mappings of gender to sex and highlight the fact that it is the relation between gender and sex that is of primary significance.

CHAPTER ONE

EMBODIMENT, CONTINGENCY,

AND AMBIGUITY

Feminists sometimes would like to talk in terms of a reversal of power. The men have had it, now we'll take the power. I don't think this is the gesture that needs to be made. It's necessary to establish a relation of two . . . two, but different from that which already exists.

—Irigaray 1995

In addition to those who would eliminate gender by arguing that so-called cultural differences are really natural, there has been a powerful tendency among feminists to empty sex of its content by arguing, conversely, that natural differences are really cultural.

—Laqueur 1990

SEXUAL DIFFERENCE AND "THE BODY"

In a rather well-known statement, Luce Irigaray maintains that sexual difference is perhaps *the* significant issue of our age (1993a, 5). Until very recently, the issue of sexual difference—and relatedly, "the body"—was neglected both by the Western philosophical tradition and by feminism's response to that tradition. Western philosophy has been a primary culprit in the establishing and maintaining of dualisms, in which the characteristics of the first terms of each dichotomous pair have been prioritized and the second terms have been rendered subordinate or invisible. Keeping with this ordering, the relation between the sexes has been defined according to a hierarchical conception of reality; men and women, or masculine and feminine, have been conceived as opposing binaries—men/masculine being traditionally prioritized over women/feminine.[1]

11

Recognizing women's subordination to men under Western dualistic thought, feminists of equality attempted to elevate women to men's position. That is, to rectify the inferior status held by women in relation to men, egalitarian feminists proposed that women should be conceived as equal to men. Women should be allowed to assume the same place as men. For Simone de Beauvoir, for example, women would ideally leave their realm of immanence to join men in their realm of transcendence.[2] In Irigaray's view, the egalitarian response to the traditional relation between the sexes is problematic in that it leaves the logic of hierarchical thought intact. Feminists of equality, rather than interrogate traditional thought, seek a solution to women's subordination and exclusion within the traditional structure itself. In the case of Beauvoir, she does not so much challenge the transcendence/ immanence dichotomy as move women from a subordinated term to a privileged one. Insofar as women's exclusion in the West is a structural, or as Genevieve Lloyd (1989) claims, a conceptual exclusion, women remain concealed when traditional frameworks are left intact. While feminists intended to improve women's situations by having them assume the privileged position, in actuality, they simply adopted a problematic structure—thereby leaving in place the mechanism of their own oppression. Women were rendered "equal" only insofar as they were depicted as "the same." Moreover, this privileged position often benefits women with class or race privilege, and it is often won at the expense of less privileged women. Ellen Messer-Davidow states that once feminists "accept the traditional framing of this matter . . . we have no way out of the system we want to change" (1989, 76).

Irigaray's concern is with the way that women have been rendered subordinate or invisible by, and within, the Western philosophical tradition. Irigaray states, "The feminine has never been defined except for the inverse, indeed the underside, of the masculine" (1985b, 146). Or as Barbara Freeman attributes to Irigaray, "[W]oman, as the possibility of a genuine sexual difference rather than one term in a binarism, does not exist in Western thought" (1988, 167). The result of a hierachical construction of the sexes is that difference in terms of binarism is not genuine difference at all; rather, it is a mere modeling of the feminine on the basis of the masculine, in accord with an economy of the same. Insofar as feminists of equality, like the tradition they criticize, have only conceived women as measured against men, they have likewise failed to think sexual difference. By seeking inclusion within a masculine standard, feminists of equality have conspired in the exclusion of feminine difference. The egalitarian approach to feminism has failed to relinquish the priority and privilege of the male model.[3]

For Irigaray, to think through the issue of sexual difference is to (re)think the relation between men and women. To think sexual difference is to think "difference" apart from hierarchy. Given that (sexual) difference has always been rendered on a hierarchical basis, to genuinely (re)think sexual difference is to reconceive the relation between traditional categories of opposition.[4] Irigaray's project, in her words, "is not to create a theory of woman, but to secure a place for the feminine within sexual difference" (1985b, 156). Unlike egalitarian feminists, Irigaray does not seek to render two terms equivalent (by conceiving the feminine as equal to the masculine) nor does she aim to valorize one term over the other (by reversing the traditional hierarchy). Irigaray says:

> In refusing or neglecting to interrogate their own categories of thought, feminists who pursue a "politics of equality" which demands not to be behind, not to be "second," are complicitious in women's exclusion from philosophy. (1995, 93)

Feminist efforts to secure a valid place for women by situating them in the privileged position ("on top") within a hierarchy is still to maintain the hierarchy. Putting women in the place where men have been merely attributes to women men's traditional location. In so doing, a genuine thinking of feminine difference—of women's "place"—remains neglected. Messer-Davidow maintains, "The mistake of many feminists . . . is reassigning traits to male and female, valorizing female and devaluing male, or shifting male and female roles" (1989, 76). The principle error is failing to question the traditional system.

Traditionally rendered, masculine and feminine difference, Irigaray claims, "has always operated 'within' systems that are representative, self-representative, of the (masculine) subject" (1985b, 159). Within such systems, the feminine has always been both absorbed and displaced by the masculine. Conceiving the feminine from its own point of view, the masculine has reduced the feminine to its own definition. Defining the feminine in masculine terms, the *feminine* has never been allowed to exist. Feminist proponents of equality maintain this same structure—as Irigaray depicts Beauvoir's position, for example: "I want to be the equal of man; I want to be the same as man; finally, I want to be a masculine subject" (1995, 99). No less problematic are feminist attempts to gain power by assuming the dominant position (that is, by reversing the hierarchy), since such efforts fail to relinquish the hierarchy itself. Different from both types of feminist program, Irigaray's project is to think "a relation of two," that is, of two [masculine and feminine] subjects.

Although men have always been attributed (or, have attributed to themselves) the role of subjects (and women of objects), underlying the traditional relation between masculine and feminine is a pretension that the subject is neutral. For instance, in prioritizing mind over body, Descartes suggests, as Susan Bordo indicates, that "given the right method, one can transcend the body" (1987, 94); "assured of his own transparency, he can relate with absolute neutrality to the objects he surveys" (95). Within Cartesian mind/body dualism, the mind is not simply juxtaposed to the body;

rather, the body must be precisely transcended for the mind (the subject) to acquire objective knowledge. To be a knowing subject is to be detached from the exterior world of objects. However, feminists such as Evelyn Fox Keller and Carol Gilligan have pointed out that this so-called objective conception of knowledge is inherently "masculinist." As masculinist, Fox Keller indicates its emphasis on "autonomy, separation, and distance" and its "radical rejection of any commingling of subject and object" (1985, 79). And Bordo claims that "Descartes' program for the purification of the understanding . . . has as its ideal the rendering *impossible* of any such continuity between subject and object" (1987, 103).[5]

Irigaray exposes as problematic the lack of a genuine relation, or of a passage, between traditional dualistic pairs—including the masculine (subject) and the feminine (object). As Irigaray emphasizes, an ontology of separation is based on a male morphology. Despite a presumed neutrality of the subject, the subject is—in fact—of the male sex/body. Although Descartes' effort was to transcend the body, his body remains the hidden element in his theorizing.[6] Irigaray's concern with such pretensions of neutrality connects her with the focus of other recent theorists of sexual difference (for example, Judith Butler, Moira Gatens, and Elizabeth Grosz) on the alleged neutrality of the body. Like women themselves, "the body" has been rendered either subordinate or invisible by, and within, the discourse of philosophy. The characteristics traditionally attributed to bodies, for example, their threat to "disrupt, erupt, overtake and overwhelm" (cf. Bordo 1987, 93), have found their corollary in the feminine. Thus, in seeking to escape the body, Western philosophy has diverted its thought from "woman" or the feminine. Similarly, feminists—in focusing on equality and sameness rather than difference—drew attention away from female bodies, since a focus on feminine, bodily difference was feared to prolong the subordination of women to men. As Elizabeth Spelman has indicated, feminism itself has fostered a profound somatophobia (cf. 1988, 120).

As a theorist of sexual difference, Irigaray seeks a relation between men and women that construes the two categories as neither essentially the same nor incommensurably opposed. Irigaray's interest in such a relation also connects with Laqueur's description of the one-sex and two-sex models of male and female bodies in *Making Sex: Body and Gender from the Greeks to Freud* (1990), since Laqueur indicates that different *interpretations* of bodies render different conceptions of the male-female relation.[7] However, Irigaray may also be viewed as rejecting both the one-sex and the two-sex models, as described by Laqueur, in that she seeks a conception of sexual difference beyond a mere reinterpretation of presumed biological facts. Theorists such as Butler, Gatens, Grosz, and Irigaray precisely question the relegation of bodies to the "natural" or the "biological" in the first place. As Laqueur's account of the one-sex and two-sex models demonstrates, male and female bodies, rather than being "brute givens," are objects subject to interpretation.

Thus, the "same" bodies (that is, women's bodies) have been rendered—at different times—both lesser versions of men's and radically distinct from men's. Gayle Rubin has pointed out that "sex as we know it . . . is itself a social product" (1975, 166), while Messer-Davidow has emphasized the concept "*ideas about* sex and gender," rather than sex/gender *traits*, in part to stress "that both phenomena are constructions" (1989, 76).

Consequently, Laqueur and others claim that the notion of the sexes as "opposed" is a cultural/historical development rather than a factual depiction of male and female bodies. "Language," Laqueur maintains, "marks this view of sexual difference" (1990, 4). One result of the idea of "opposing sexes," in Laqueur's view, is that "sexuality as a singular and all-important human attribute with a specific object—the *opposite* sex—is the product of the late eighteenth century" (1990, 13). He concludes, "There is nothing natural about it" (13). And as Rubin has suggested, "Gender is not only an identification with one sex; it also entails that sexual desire be directed toward the other sex" (1975, 180). A particular conception or interpretation of the relationship between male and female *bodies* is thereby linked to a certain notion of sexual desire. As the sexes are conceived as oppositional, the object of desire is constructed as the purported opposite sex. As a "given" sex is considered to entail a specific gender, that sex is likewise thought to demand a specific object of desire. "Desire" is thereby implicated in different views—or models—of the relation between male and female bodies.

Whereas on the one-sex model, women are thought to be atrophied variations of men; on the two-sex model, women are interpreted to be qualitatively distinct from men. Sexual difference, or the relation between the sexes, is rendered on the basis of "degree" in the one instance versus "kind" in the other. Around the year 1800, Laqueur claims:

> In place of what strikes the modern imagination as an almost perverse insistence on understanding sexual difference as a matter of degree, gradations of one basic male type, there arose a shrill call to articulate sharp corporeal distinctions. . . . Sexual difference in kind, not degree, seemed solidly grounded in nature. (Laqueur 1990, 5–6)

The very notion of sexual difference as "grounded in nature" led egalitarian feminists to de-emphasize women's difference(s) from men and to stress their likeness(es) to them. That is, feminists upheld a wariness of "difference" between the sexes and retreated from "the body," since bodies were understood to link women with an unalterable nature—and "nature" was considered responsible for maintaining women's subordination to men. By moving away from bodies, feminists adopted—or took as obvious—an articulation of bodies as natural, given, static, and factual.

However, for feminist theorists of sexual difference, to think through the issue of sexual difference is to bring into question the very notion of bodies as "factual" or "natural" at all. Such theorists do not limit or essentialize women by placing them "in" their bodies, as they have sometimes been accused of doing. Instead of suggesting that women transcend their bodies, sexual difference theorists locate the possibility of women's movement in an interrogation of bodies themselves. Rather than promoting an overcoming of bodies (the same type of transcendence argued, for men, by traditional philosophy), their aim is to confront bodies in their usual renderings. Hence, "the body" central to feminist theories of sexual difference is not the body as traditionally conceived. While the Western tradition has overwhelmingly neglected bodies as worthy topics of investigation, bodies—when they *have* been considered—have been theorized as restricting, confining, and impeding. It is not until recently that they have been thought otherwise.

CONTINGENCY, NON-NEUTRALITY, SEX/GENDER

Neglect or distrust of bodies, as suggested above, has been prevalent in feminism and has infected the feminist distinction between sex and gender. Genevieve Lloyd indicates, for example, that part of the problem with the sex-gender distinction as traditionally conceived by feminists is that the "distinction itself brings with it many of the difficulties inherent in Descartes' way of conceptualizing the relation between mind and body" (1989, 19). Bodies, or sexes, have been considered "independent of processes of socialisation," while minds, or genders, have been rendered "complete unto themselves" (Lloyd 1989, 19).[8] The Cartesian mind-body relation, like the feminist sex-gender distinction, is a relation in which "bodily differences lie entirely outside the realm of mind" or gender—"causally interacting with it, but separate from it" (19). In separating mind from body, gender from sex, mind/body and gender/sex are established to relate only arbitrarily. Confined to their own distinctive and mutually exclusive realms, neither mind/body nor gender/sex need seemingly relate at all. The connection between femininity (gender) and the female body (sex) is depicted as merely accidental. Thus, feminists have claimed that female bodies are capable of assuming masculine traits (a different gender), enabling women to engage in an equal relation with men. However, residing behind this conceptualization of the sex-gender distinction is the problematic assumption that the body is neutral.

In "A Critique of the Sex/Gender Distinction," Gatens states, "Concerning the neutrality of the body, let me be explicit, there is no neutral body, there are at least two kinds of bodies; the male body and the female body" (1991, 145). Gatens's claim against assumptions of bodies as neutral is a claim against, what she calls, "the postulated *arbitrary* connection between femininity and the female body; masculinity and the male body" (1991, 140). Gatens suggests, in a way comparable to Irigaray, that it is the relation between categories that must be interrogated. In the case of Gatens, it is a certain presumed relation between femininity and female bodies, masculinity and male bodies, that proves problematic. While the traditional conception of the relation between sex and gender has been one of necessity—that is, masculinity has been conceived to attach to male bodies, femininity to female bodies, by a sort of ontological necessity—feminist programs of degendering have, on the other hand, attempted to elevate women to men's equals by proposing that women, like men, are capable of assuming masculine characteristics. While on the traditional conception of their relation, sex and gender collapse (they merge by way of a presumed ontological necessity), on feminist proposals of degendering, sex and gender strictly divide (they are conceived to relate only arbitrarily). Bodies are presumed to be neutral, allowing the application of either masculine or feminine characteristics. At the forefront of Gatens's critique is the presumed arbitrariness of the relation between the categories of sex and gender. What occurs in-between the bodies discussed by Gatens—the male body and the female body—marks the site of a new critical examination.

For Irigaray, both the traditional and the degendering views of the sex-gender relation or distinction would be mistaken. On the traditional view, gender is absorbed into sex; the difference between gender and sex is neutralized. On the degendering view, gender displaces sex; gender is prioritized to the exclusion of sex. In a similar manner, Anne Edwards remarks that the "overwhelming preoccupation with the socially constructed differences and divisions between men and women . . . has inevitably resulted in gender getting all the attention and sex being largely forgotten" (1989, 7). "Until very recently," Edwards continues, "the original equation of sex with biology, as something pregiven and non-social remained unquestioned" (7). Feminists neglected sex, or emptied sex of content and focused on gender, since sex—like the body—was presumed to be simply given or neutral. In the words of Gatens, sex was conceived as a "barren category" (1991, 139). The category *gender* appeared a more fruitful one for feminist purposes. Lack of attention to sex, by feminists, parallels lack of concern with the body by Western philosophy in general. Bodies, as Grosz points out, have "remained a conceptual blind spot" (1994, 3). Likewise, Laqueur emphasizes, "The presence of the body is so veiled as to be almost hidden" (1990, 12). And Braidotti remarks, "In a lot of ways, the body is the dark continent of feminist thought" (1994, 180).

In addition to Gatens's critique, the presumed neutral status of bodies has been the focus of Butler and Grosz. Their analyses assume the following form: for Grosz, social, historical, and cultural factors do not merely impinge on *pregiven* bodies; rather, such factors actively produce bodies as of a "determinate type" (1994, x). Grosz places bodies at the center of analysis, not in an attempt to reduce subjectivity to bodies, but in an effort to explain the effects of subjectivity "using the subject's corporeality as a framework" (1994, vii). She undermines dualistic views of the subject (that is, the idea that minds and bodies are two separate, unconnected sorts of "stuff") by discussing both how the subject's "psychical interior" acts to form a body as a specific type of exteriority (from the inside out), and how "social inscriptions" on the body's surface serve to produce a psychical interiority (from the outside in). Grosz demonstrates how bodies, of their very "nature," are amenable to social organization and completion; that is to say, how bodies are volatile. In their volatility, bodies are located in-between "inner" and "outer"—marking the locus of connection between the psychical and the social.

Like Grosz, Butler (1993) argues that gender is not a cultural overlay or construct imposed on a given sex or body. Such a view is problematic, Butler claims, since (in language comparable to Irigaray's) gender so conceived "absorbs and displaces" sex (5). Sex is construed as a factual/static state of the subject's body which is, in effect, cancelled by the social meaning assumed by gender. By contrast, Butler maintains that the concept of sex is itself problematic. Sex is not a pregiven object, but is instead an ideal construct. It is, in Butler's view, a "regulatory ideal" in the Foucauldian sense. "Regulatory power" is not an external imposition of "power" on a subject but is an operative constraint in the subject's very formation. For Butler, the materiality of bodies (or, the category *sex*) is both "constructed" by, and resistant to, social/historical/cultural influences. Bodies are not simply given; instead, they are "forcibly materialized through time" (Butler 1993, 1). Thus, sex is not merely a factual/natural category. It is, rather, a "cultural norm" governing bodies and their materialization. This implies that sex is not only a malleable—or volatile—category, but that it is a normative one. Sex (as it regulates bodies) resides in-between construction and constraint.

On this point, Butler can be brought into dialogue with Gatens, since Gatens argues against feminist programs of degendering that conceive sex as a biological category and gender as a social one, and claim that women can attain equality with men through a resocialization of gender roles. In Gatens's view, such programs uncritically assume that "the body is neutral and passive with regard to the formation of consciousness," and that "the important effects of the historical and cultural specificity of one's 'lived experience' is able to be altered . . . by consciously changing the material practices of the culture in question" (1991, 143). For Gatens, it is significant that cultures do not simply valorize masculinity, for example. She states, "It is not masculinity *per se* that is valorized in our culture but the masculine male" (151). Since, as Gatens indicates, "a network of relations [normative relations] obtain between femininity and femaleness, that is, between the female *body* and femininity," there is likewise "a qualitative difference between the kind of femininity 'lived' by men" (146). Again, for Gatens, the relation between such categories must be examined.

In agreement with Gatens, Grosz claims that gender cannot be construed as an ideological category imposed on a biological foundation. That is, if bodies are not natural facts as has been supposed, but are themselves volatile, then gender can no longer be conceived as a malleable overlay on a static category *sex*. To (re)think bodies is, thus, to rethink the distinction/relation between gender and sex. Like Gatens, Grosz maintains that genders cannot be neutrally ascribed to bodies. The masculinity of male bodies is not the same as the masculinity of female bodies. In the words of Grosz, the kind of body matters in the "meaning and function of gender that emerges" (1994, 58).

One consequence of Grosz's focus on bodies, as she herself notes, is that it allows the question of sexual difference to be framed in new ways. Through an investigation of bodies, Grosz states that questions of women's sexual specificity can be raised to more readily "demonstrate and problematize" the social subordination of women to men. Grosz brings sexual difference to the forefront, showing how an investigation of bodies must also be an investigation of bodies as sexed. In a way similar to Grosz, Gatens indicates that programs of degendering neutralize sexual difference by proposing "sexual equality" through relearning what are taken to be arbitrary gender roles. However, if the human subject is conceived in sexually specific terms, then in Gatens's view, "patriarchy" is not properly conceived as "a system of social organization that valorizes the masculine *gender* over the feminine gender. Gender is not the issue," Gatens states, "sexual difference is" (1991, 145).

For Irigaray, as with Gatens and Grosz, the rethought relation between sex and gender is neither one of necessity nor of arbitrariness; it is, rather, one of contingency. Irigaray's thinking through sexual difference is, again, a thinking of difference—the difference between sex and gender included—to foster alliance without absorption. The type of relation that can both preserve and mediate difference is precisely a contingent one. Whereas the traditional view of the relation between sex and gender erred in relating sex and gender necessarily, feminist responses to the traditional view, in the form of degendering programs, failed in conceiving the relation as purely arbitrary. This is to say that while masculinity has been traditionally conceived as the only logical outcome of male bodies (and femininity of female bodies), feminists mistakenly took the opposing view, claiming *no* correspondence between gender and sex. By detaching gender from sex, feminists— like the tradition, albeit in an opposing way from the tradition—neglected the significance of sex and its relation to gender. If subjectivity can be explained on the basis of corporeality while not being reducible to it, as Grosz suggests, then the subject neither passively adopts a natural, given gender nor actively assumes a gender unrelated to sex or the body. Rather, the subject resides at the intersection of—in-between—natural/biological sex and cultural/social gender (cf. Braidotti 1994, 182). The subject is neither a passive surface nor an active, unrestrained site. In this respect, the bodies at the center of feminist analyses of sexual difference are bodies as lived; that is, bodies that reside in-between nature and culture.

To say that the relation between sex and gender must be understood as "contingent" means that although male bodies tend to adopt masculine traits (or female bodies, feminine ones), this mapping of sex to gender is not a required or necessary one. For example, male bodies can, and sometimes do, assume traditionally feminine traits (and vice versa). The very ability of bodies to assume "unexpected" characteristics defeats the claim that sex causes gender. Moreover, the traditional notion that sex and gender are necessarily or naturally linked translates into relegating such cases of unexpected gender assumption to the heading *unnatural*. Such unnaturalness is precisely born of a faulty assumption vis-à-vis sex and gender. Thus, as Butler claims, "oppressive gender norms continue to exist only to the extent that they are taken up and given life again and again" (1986, 41). The mistake of egalitarian or degendering feminists is failing to recognize the normative nature of the category *sex*; that is, neglecting the fact that different meanings are attributed to various mappings of sex to gender. Some of these mappings are promoted while others are "prohibited." On a theory of sexual difference, these very mappings—or relations between—are examined.

AMBIGUITY AND BODIES

Irigaray argues that by relegating women to bodies, men (or the Western tradition) have attempted to contain and control them. Bodies, depicted as capable of overwhelming subjects (where "subjects" are located in "minds"), have been rendered sites of needed restraint. Spelman, among others, has pointed out that "the body is seen as an enormous and annoying obstacle"— threatening to "get the upper hand over the soul" (1988, 113). Linking women with bodies thereby means attributing to women the required restraint of bodies. However, insofar as women have been associated with bodies, and insofar as the question of "woman" or of sexual difference has not been thought, it is also the case that the body has not been genuinely thought. "The body that gives life," Irigaray states, "never enters into language" (1993b, 46). Although it serves as a starting point (for him), the maternal-feminine nonetheless remains unthought (by him). "This sameness," Irigaray remarks, "is the maternal-feminine which has been assimilated before any perception of difference. . . . It is this sameness that constitutes the subject as a living being but that man has not begun to think: his body" (1993a, 98).

In *her* effort to (re)think "the body," Butler states:

> I found that I could not fix bodies as simple objects of thought. Not only did bodies tend to indicate a world beyond themselves, but this movement beyond their own boundaries . . . appeared to be quite central to what bodies "are." (1993, ix)

"It is this ability of bodies to always extend the frameworks which attempt to contain them," Grosz maintains, "which fascinates me" (1994, xi). While the attempt, traditionally, has been to confine bodies, bodies of their very nature appear to resist or defy such limitation. Whereas bodies have been purportedly kept under control or "put in their place" by Western philosophical frameworks, to theorize bodies means to recognize their entrance into places where access has been presumably denied. Grosz claims, "Sexual difference is a mobile, indeed, volatile, concept, able to insinuate itself into regions where it should have no place" (1994, ix). If, rather than being neutral and static, bodies bleed—extend or exceed frameworks—then men, in relegating women to the bodily in an attempt to contain them, have actually placed women in an "unlimited site." If bodily boundaries are ambiguous (which is not to say arbitrary), then women, like bodies, resist and alter a static definition. Irigaray claims, "[He] places limits on her that are the opposite of the unlimited site in which he unwittingly situates her" (1993a, 11). Contrary to men's attempts to limit women (for example, by placing women "in" their bodies), women confound confinement in virtue of this very placement. "The body is a most peculiar 'thing,' " Grosz says, "for it is never quite reducible to being merely a thing; nor does it manage to rise above the status of thing. Thus, it is both a thing and a non-thing" (1994, xi).

Butler (1993) makes a similar point to Grosz in conceiving "matter" not simply as a passive surface but as a dynamic site. In "Sex and Gender in Simone de Beauvoir's *Second Sex*," Butler indicates that "[b]y purposely embodying ambiguity—dichotomies lose their forcefulness" (1986, 327). Despite what has been described as Beauvoir's problematic conceptualization of sex and gender vis-à-vis bodies, implicit within Beauvoir's account—as Butler brings out—is a productive sense of "ambiguity." The problem with Beauvoir's rendering of the sex-gender distinction is that gender, in the words of Butler, "becomes a free-floating artifice" (1990, 6). Gender, to reiterate, is "theorized as radically independent of sex" (6). Such a division between sex and gender produces the difficulty highlighted by Gatens and is articulated by Butler as follows: "[T]he consequence [is] that *man* and the *masculine* might just as easily signify a female body as a male one, and *woman* and the *feminine* a male body as easily as a female one" (1990, 6). The female body becomes the "*arbitrary locus* of the gender 'woman' " (Butler 1986, 35). Again, this arbitrariness is problematic in its neglect of bodies, in its assumption that bodies are simply neutral. Beauvoir's well-known claim in *The Second Sex* is that "[o]ne is not born, but rather becomes, a woman." Revealed in this statement is the problematic separation of sex from gender; but also demonstrated, in more productive terms, is an ambiguity involving the verb *become* (Butler 1986, 36). Butler maintains that, within Beauvoir's account, gender assumption is both a "project" and a "construct"; it is "a purposeful set of acts" and "a received cultural construction" (1986, 36). Gender assumption or "choosing a gender," according to Butler, means "to interpret received gender-norms in a way that organizes them anew" (1986, 40). This conception of gender (1986) prefigures Butler's account of "matter" (1993) as being both produced/constructed and resistant to production/construction. Like the ambiguity involved in becoming a gender, a certain ambiguity involving matter places it in-between traditional terms of opposition. To be ambiguous, or to be in an ambiguous position, is to interrogate the mandates of "fit" instituted by categories of mutual exclusion.

Irigaray's interest in certain Greek mythological figures introduces a comparable point. For example, in her reading of Diotima's discourse in Plato's *Symposium*, Irigaray shows Diotima's nature to be one of essential ambiguity. By rendering the relation between pairs of opposites ambiguous, and by embodying ambiguity herself, Diotima introduces a relation between oppositional pairs different from that of traditional binaries. Commentators on the *Symposium* have, however, tended to interpret Diotima's discourse as presenting Plato's view of love (*eros*). The notion that *eros* is intermediary, or ambiguous, between opposites has been neglected in favor of a Platonic formulation of desire—a formulation in which desire is subjected to a telos. In a similar manner, Irigaray suggests that the figure of Antigone, from Sophocles' play, "is silenced in her action. Locked up—paralyzed, on the edge of the city. Because she is neither master nor slave. And this upsets the order of the dialectic" (1993a, 119). Irigaray refers to Hegel, who, as a commentator on the *Antigone*, interprets Antigone according to her "properly feminine role"—thus limiting her. Irigaray argues that Antigone actually *confounds* the dialectic by refusing her assigned position. Antigone, that is, bleeds her defined boundary within Hegel's system. And of Persephone, Irigaray says, "Persephone does not stand still. . . . She passes, ceaselessly, from the (male/female) ones to the others, but she knows their differences" (1991, 114). Like bodies, whose borders are unclear, "[Persephone] . . . passes beyond all boundaries" (115). Persephone refuses to be contained.

With the introduction of ambiguity—with the opening of a passage between opposites rather than the lack of alliance accorded a strict divide— the traditional view of "difference" gets recast. Speaking of sexual difference, Irigaray states, "We must examine our history thoroughly to understand why this sexual difference has not had its chance to develop. . . . It is surely a question of the dissociation of the body and soul . . . of the lack of a passage" (1993a, 15). "As for philosophy," she continues:

> So far as the question of woman is concerned—and it comes down to the question of sexual difference—this is indeed what has to be brought into question. . . . The philosophical order is indeed one that has to be questioned, and *disturbed*, inasmuch as it covers over sexual difference. (1985b, 150)

The figures that concern Irigaray throughout her works—in a way comparable to Butler's discussion of the resistance of matter—resist and disturb, in the words of Grosz, "the frameworks which attempt to contain them" (1994, xi). By disturbing traditional frameworks, these figures act to reveal the very issue of sexual difference. The ability of certain figures to expose sexual difference, or bodies, demonstrates that although the issue of sexual difference has been concealed by the Western philosophical tradition, it is none-theless resistant to a complete "forgetting." The issue of sexual difference is, at moments, revealed in the precise texts that neglect it.

Consequently, Irigaray must be read through her claim of sexual differ-ence, and sexual difference should be understood in the manner outlined above. In so doing, Irigaray's readings can be given a proper context. Readers of Irigaray have, at times, failed to do this. For example, by failing to con-sider Irigaray's concern with sexual difference, Andrea Nye (1992) misunder-stands the intent of Irigaray's reading of Diotima's discourse in Plato's *Symposium*. Nye underestimates the value that Irigaray places on the figure of Diotima and fails to see the movement that Diotima's discourse depicts, for Irigaray, within the history of Western metaphysics. Similarly, by failing to take Irigaray's concern with sexual difference as a long-standing concern, Luisa Murara (1994) argues that Irigaray's work shifts with the essay, "The Universal as Mediation," from a focus on women-to-women (mother-daughter) relations to men-to-women (sexually different) relations. Although Irigaray's work may mark shifts, her concern with sexual difference can be traced throughout her works and is consistently central to her readings. Such femi-nist (mis)readings of Irigaray illustrate the same basic point that Irigaray herself makes with respect to the Western philosophical tradition: "These mediators [Diotima and Antigone]," Irigaray states, "are often forgotten" (1993a, 106). It is in their role as intermediaries (that is, as "angels" gestur-ing toward possibilities that have not yet been allowed to manifest) that Irigaray intends to illuminate such figures. By reading Irigaray in terms of the issue of sexual difference, and by connecting Irigaray with recent feminist scholarship on the status of the body, these figures may be revealed in their forgotten role as mediators—intermediaries who bridge binaries.

Additionally, inasmuch as Irigaray's claim of sexual difference is an ontological claim; that is, one that interrogates traditional Western meta-physics, Irigaray is concerned to open and reveal difference broadly con-strued. Irigaray locates the possibility of a genuine relation of difference—a difference that is non-hierarchically ordered—in a fundamental consider-ation of sexual difference in Western thought. Hence, in a statement that could pertain to Irigaray, Gatens states:

> Many feminists have argued that those representations of women cannot be dismissed as superficial bias on the part of (predomi-nantly) male theorists. Rather, it has been argued that those repre-sentations have a metaphysical basis in Western thought that is not easily removed without destroying the coherence of the philosophi-cal system concerned. (1996, vii)[9]

By considering Irigaray's concern with sexual difference as an approach, her thinking of sexual difference can be interpreted as a thinking intended to disturb and "to lay foundations different from" those of the tradition (1993a, 6). By interrogating the structure of Western thought—or, by positing how sexual difference unsettles that structure—other forms of difference can like-wise be engaged. Again, the essential neglect of Western philosophy has been that of bodies. While presumably being written out of philosophy, bodies emerge to affect and to show themselves within it. Consequently, the pursuit of disembodiment is a fundamentally flawed endeavor since the pres-ence of the body can never really be denied.[10]

CHAPTER TWO

IRIGARAY'S (RE)FIGURING OF

SPACE-TIME AND PLACE

Again and again, taking from the feminine the tissue or the texture of spatiality. In exchange—but it isn't a real one—he buys her a house, even shuts her up in it, places limits on her that are the opposite of the unlimited site in which he unwittingly situates her.

—Irigaray 1993a

Just as the scar of the navel is forgotten. . . . The womb is never thought of as the primal place in which we become body.

—Irigaray 1993b

THE APPROACH OF SEXUAL DIFFERENCE

When Irigaray offers her readings of Plato and Aristotle in *An Ethics of Sexual Difference*, she does not concentrate on their political thought in the *Republic* and the *Politics*, as one might expect. Instead, she focuses on Diotima's discourse on love/desire (*eros*) in the *Symposium* and the treatise on "place" in *Physics* IV. Perhaps Irigaray provides her readings because feminists have neglected the *Symposium* and the *Physics*, but a more likely and specific source of motivation involves the reason *why* feminists have taken the *Republic* and the *Politics* as texts ripe for feminist discussion. Insofar as egalitarian feminists have taken as their concern the issue of securing women's equality with men, when reading texts of the Western tradition, they have aimed to locate occasions of such equality. While an equality of the sexes has been found in Plato's conception of the ideal state, for example, it has been considered lacking in Aristotle's relegation of women to the home on the basis of "natural" difference. As Alison Jaggar indicates, "The dominant theme in the modern western debate over the place of women in society has been the tension between the ideal of sexual equality and the apparent reality of sexual difference" (1990, 239).[1] Standard feminist critiques of Plato and Aristotle, themselves operating within modern Western debate, have come to illustrate a more general concern with the issue of equality versus difference.

Early in the process of feminist reflection on the Western tradition, Susan Moller Okin stated that "[n]o one has yet examined systematically the treatment of women in the classic works of political philosophy" (1979, 3). Assuming this task, Okin focused on two central questions: "Whether the existing tradition of political philosophy can sustain the inclusion of women in its subject matter?" and "Whether the philosophers' arguments about the nature of women and their proper place, viewed within the context of their complete political theories, will help [one] to understand why a substantial equality between the sexes" has failed to ensue (Okin 1979, 4). These questions, which exemplify subsequent feminist concern with women and Western philosophy, emphasize the issues of women's inclusion (or equality) within existing social/political frameworks and women's "nature" (or difference) as a possible source of exclusion from these structures. These questions focus on women's equality with men versus their differences from them—vis-à-vis a predetermined (that is, man-made) realm of politics. The questions effectively ask: Can women fit within what exists?, where "what exists" refers first and foremost to a political system. When reading the canon, feminists have overwhelmingly selected texts and concentrated on aspects of those texts with such questions as Okin's in mind—the questions themselves being cast by, or presuming, a certain conception of "feminism."

In examining Plato's *Republic* and Aristotle's *Politics*, Nicholas Smith has suggested that feminists have read Plato as representing " 'one of the few notable exceptions' in our long history of sexism, whereas Aristotle [has been interpreted as] . . . 'a dangerous chauvinist' " (1983, 486). This view is supported by the fact that Plato, in the *Republic*, "argues that women must be assigned social roles in the ideal state equal (or approximate) to those of men," while "Aristotle, in his *Politics*, returns women to their traditional roles in the home, serving men" (Smith 1983, 467).[2] In Irigaray's view, the aim of equalizing traditional hierarchical frameworks and obliterating difference (since difference with respect to sex has been thought to represent a "dangerous" position) has meant that feminists have concealed a genuine thinking of sexual difference. Equality has been conflated with sameness, and the issue of women's exclusion has "remained at the level of critical demands" (Irigaray 1993a, 6). Wanting to be equal to men, women remain defined only in relation to masculine subjects. Consequently, feminist readings of Plato and Aristotle have not departed from "traditional categories of logic and understanding" (1995, 100). Irigaray states, "Claims that men, races, sexes, are equal in point of fact signal a disdain or denial for real phenomena and give rise to an imperialism even more pernicious than those that retain traces of difference" (1993b, vi). We need an ethics based on identity, Irigaray suggests, not equality (cf. 1993b, vi).[3] That is, we need an ethics attendant to differences rather than one that universalizes humans as the same. Thus, it is not at all clear that Plato is to be preferred over Aristotle, especially on the premise of a purported equality over difference. It is the very ideal of sexual equality, on which much of feminism has been premised, that Irigaray calls into question.

In Irigaray's view, women's exclusion has not occurred first and foremost in the realm of politics or biology, but at the level of ontology. Women's exclusion is primarily a metaphysical one. Hence, to enact progress at the political level, feminists must examine the very foundations on which [political] thought has been constructed. By failing to question its own categories of thought, Irigaray suggests, feminism actually conspires in the exclusion of women from philosophy. "Using the same ground and the same framework as 'first philosophy,'" she claims, feminists fail to propose "any other goals that might assume new foundations and new works" (Irigaray 1993a, 6). For Irigaray, like Bordo (1987) and others, feminism has remained within a Cartesian mind/body dualism whereby an ideal of equality has presumed a certain neutrality of subjects (of consciousnesses or minds), and the reality of sexual difference has referred to an assumed givenness of bodies. By failing to take bodies seriously themselves, feminists have fostered their own suspicion of the body and have reduced the category *sex* to a biological, static, neutral position. As a result, feminism has operated on the basis of a gendered, metaphysical division. For Irigaray, sexual difference represents an underlying and foundational issue; it is an issue that opens and interrogates traditional structures and frameworks (1993a, 5). With respect to metaphysics, this means to rethink the basic categories of reality.

IRIGARAY'S THINKING THROUGH SPACE-TIME

Crucial to Irigaray's rethinking of traditional metaphysical categories is a reconceptualization of space and time—a concept that Irigaray renders "space-time" (1993a, 7). The traditional Western view of space and time has rendered women subordinate to men through associating women with space and men with time. For instance, women (as mothers) have been relegated to maternity (space), while men (as God) have been linked to eternity (time). If women have been traditionally linked with space, or the spatial, then a particular view of women's bodies can be found to support this connection. Women, conceived in terms of "lack" or "emptiness," for example, have been thought to provide space for men (in sexual acts) or children (in reproductive ones). Women are depicted as receptacles, as the passive sites for men's activities. To say that men have been traditionally associated with time, or the temporal, is also to say that time—conceptualized as "projection"—relates time to men's bodies or a male morphology. Men's anatomies, in other words, can be understood as "projected"—as inserted into space. Consequently, women, conceived as empty space, provide the place for men's bodies or forms. Despite the conceptual attachment of space and time to female and male morphologies, the categories of space and time have nevertheless been taken to be neutral. That is, they have been considered factual depictions of a given reality, unrelated to and unencumbered by bodies or sexual difference.

In considering Irigaray's reading of Diotima's discourse in Plato's *Symposium*, Irigaray's concern with reconceiving space and time must be brought to bear upon her analysis. Irigaray states, "The transition to a new age [of sexual difference] comes at the same time as a change in the economy of desire" and the interval *between* (1993a, 8; my emphasis). "Desire," Irigaray maintains, "occupies or designates the place of the interval" (8).[4] In her reading of Diotima's discourse, Irigaray thematizes the link between *eros* and space-time. On the subject of *eros* in the *Symposium*, Irigaray states, "Love is designated as the theme, but love is also perpetually enacted and dramatized, in the exposition of the theme" (1992, 65). I likewise maintain that sexual difference, although not specified as the dialogue's theme or even as the theme of Irigaray's reading, is nonetheless dramatized by the very discourse of Diotima. The issue of sexual difference can be seen, in other words, to implicitly parallel the *Symposium*'s explicit theme of love. Insofar as "a genuine thinking of sexual difference" requires a transformation of basic categories of reality, such as space and time, the figure of Diotima represents a path toward this reconception.

The Symposium's Dramatic Context: Diotima's Status

To think through the issue of sexual difference, for Irigaray, is neither to grant priority to one sex over the other (whereby difference is rendered in hierarchical fashion) nor to posit an androgynous relation (whereby difference is subordinated to a conceived sameness of the sexes). Rather, to (re)think sexual difference is to (re)conceive the relation between men and women in terms other than traditional/oppositional difference, on the one hand, or androgynous/symmetrical sameness, on the other hand.

An essentially androgynous relation between the sexes is depicted in the *Symposium* itself, in the speech of Aristophanes. Here, Aristophanes states:

> First of all, you must learn the constitution of man and the modifications which it has undergone, for originally it was different from what it is now. In the first place there were three sexes, not, as with us, two, male and female; the third partook of the nature of both the others and has vanished. (187E)[5]

Perturbed by the strength and arrogance of the original third-sexed creature, Zeus decides to split each creature in two. In this way, he thinks he can ensure the continuation of the human race while putting "an end to their wickedness by making them weaker" (190D). Having divided the creatures in half, the story continues, Zeus asks Apollo to turn their faces to the cut side of their bodies and to heal their wounds. Apollo "smoothed out the wrinkles but left a few on the belly round the navel, to remind man of the state from which he had fallen" (191A). The navel serves as a reminder of this traumatic separation—a separation through which, as Laqueur indicates, "[s]exual difference came about as the representation in the flesh of the fall from grace" (1990, 7). Thus, sexual difference is depicted as derivative of a more original human condition, while the navel marks the point of both connection and detachment in-between bodies.

Through the division of the original creature, the two sexes become constituted as opposing elements—related by way of an underlying sameness. Aristophanes uses the story of the third-sexed creature to provide an account of love. As he states, "Man's original body having thus been cut in two, each half yearned for the half from which it had been severed" (191B). "Originally we were whole beings," says Aristophanes, "before our wickedness caused us to be separated by Zeus" (192D). Therefore, "Love is simply the desire and pursuit of the whole" (192E). On Aristophanes' account, love serves to reunite opposing masculine and feminine elements in a condition of original androgyny.

When Diotima's views on love are presented in the *Symposium*, through the mouth of Socrates, there are several allusions to the earlier speech of Aristophanes. Diotima says, for example:

> There is indeed a theory that lovers are people who are in search of the other half of themselves, but according to my view of the matter, love is not desire either of the half or of the whole. (203A)

Within this context, Diotima's rejection of Aristophanes' view of love can be taken as a denial that love serves a sort of unifying function. Diotima thereby anticipates a vision of love other than such a blending of difference. As Irigaray points out, love serves to *mediate* between pairs of opposites: mortality and immortality, ignorance and knowledge, poverty and plenty, etc. (1992, 68). For Diotima, "love is half-way between mortal and immortal" (205E); it is, as Irigaray states, "a space-time of permanent *passage*" (71). Love is a "great spirit," according to Diotima, and in the nature of all spirits, is "half-god and half-man" (202E). The function of such beings is "to interpret and convey messages to the gods from men and to men from the gods" (202E). "Being of an intermediate nature, a spirit bridges the gap between . . . [gods and men], and prevents the universe from falling into two separate halves" (202E). A spirit offers a link between bodies. In Diotima's speech, the role of love is not to unite men and women in a state of sameness; rather, it is to preserve and mediate their difference(s).[6]

The features that Diotima attributes to love, Socrates likewise attributes to love, Socrates likewise attributes to Diotima. Not only is love a spirit, but so is Diotima herself. Socrates characterizes her as having postponed the plague for ten years (201D). Although the Athenians had offered sacrifices in an attempt to avert the plague, it was Diotima who had succeeded. This suggests that Diotima is to be viewed as a figure "above" human beings (in her ability to deter certain events), but at the same time, she is to be viewed as someone "below" the gods (in her inability to avoid these events altogether). She is to be viewed, that is, as intermediate between men and gods—she moves *in-between* mortal and immortal—for even though she succeeded in postponing the plague, she nonetheless did not prevent the plague altogether. As Irigaray states, "*angels* . . . circulate as mediators of that which has not yet happened, of what is still going to happen, of what is on the horizon" (1993a, 15). Diotima is a guide, as Martha Nussbaum indicates. She is someone capable of moving the Athenians away from the plague and other maladies if they will only listen (1986, 177). Diotima is a guide in the sense that love, Irigaray remarks, "is both the guide and the way, above all a mediator" (1992, 65). Irigaray maintains that the angel is "yet to be made manifest in the realm of time and space" (15).

Lacking a mediator, an intermediary, a spirit, an angel, "[e]verything remains separate, even opposed to one another" (Irigaray 1993a, 15). There had been no intermediary in the case of Aristophanes' third-sexed creature to deter Zeus from splitting the beings into halves. There had been no mediator to prevent the separation of an original being into masculine and feminine elements. The reference to Aristophanes' speech suggests that Diotima is introduced as a figure able to serve as intermediary. In turn, her own role of intermediary serves to exemplify Diotima's views on love (that love, too, is of an intermediate nature). In its role as mediator, love is not simply a means to a greater, separate end; rather, love is already there *within* the pairs of opposites and is unveiled as a third term—one that "permits progression to a greater perfection of and in love" (Irigaray 1992, 64). "[Diotima] speaks—in a style that is loosely *woven* but never definitely knotted—of becoming in time" (Irigaray 1992, 71).

Itself the offspring of the oppositions of *Poverty* (his mother) and *Plenty* (his Father), love has features of both. Irigaray states:

> Love is always poor and rough, unkempt, unshod, and homeless . . . because he has the nature of his mother. But again, in keeping with his father, he has designs upon the beautiful and the good. (66)

Halfway between *Poverty* and *Plenty*, love serves to mediate their opposition; "love is a *demon*," Irigaray says—"a being of middling nature" (66). Having Diotima refer to Aristophanes' speech therefore suggests that "Diotima" is employed within the dialogue to fulfill a certain dramatic function. Just as Plato has Socrates ask Diotima the function of a spirit, such as love (202E),

Diotima is herself offered as an example of a spirit. The references to Aristophanes' speech not only corroborate the status of Diotima (and love) as intermediary, they also indicate that Socrates is not recounting Diotima's view from an actual, previous conversation.[7] This indication runs counter to Socrates' explicit claim that "I will try to give the best consecutive account I can of what she told me" (201E), and suggests that statements made within the context of the dialogue must be considered from within that context. Diotima's dramatic function is, moreover, suggested by her very name. As Martha Nussbaum states:

> "Diotima" simply means "Zeus-honor" and would in all likelihood have been construed by Plato as ambiguous between "the one who gives honor to Zeus" and "the one who receives honor from Zeus." (1986, 177, ftn 28)

It is the ambiguity of her name that even more fully suggests the intermediate nature of Diotima herself; for she does not simply bestow honor on Zeus, she likewise receives his honor. Diotima is neither lover nor beloved; rather, she is placed in-between. Her nature is one of essential ambiguity. Again, Diotima is like love in that love, Irigaray says, "is a constantly moving intermediary"; love is "neither lover nor beloved, but both" (1992, 65).[8]

While this reconception of love enters discussion in virtue of Diotima, it is not Diotima herself who speaks these views. Rather, the alleged views of Diotima have been placed in the mouth of Socrates. Perhaps most important, then, to a consideration of Diotima's discourse is a recognition that "the 'speech of Diotima' [is] a speech of Socrates" (Taylor 1966, 225).[9]

Presence and Absence: Diotima's "Miscarriage"

Irigaray claims that Socrates attributes Diotima with two incompatible views, borrowed here in formulation from Eleanor Kuykendall: (1) "that love is a midpoint or intermediary between lovers" (as has been seen above), and (2) "that love is a means to the end and duty of procreation" whereby the "intermediary becomes the child, and [is] no longer love" (1992, 60 and 64). Irigaray maintains that, with the arrival of the second view (*Symposium*, 206), Diotima's method "miscarries" (1993a, 70).

Irigaray's use of "miscarries" (*échoue*) is significant, since "miscarries" has the sense of "to come to harm," "to go wrong," "to go amiss." Diotima's method, Irigaray implies, has been somewhat actively disengaged, diverted, expelled.[10] The significance of the word *miscarries* for Irigaray is reflected when she cautions her readers that the speech of Diotima is a speech of Socrates. Irigaray reminds her readers of this more than once, indicating that she is suspicious of the way Socrates sometimes renders Diotima's alleged views. Irigaray states on two occasions, for example, that "[Diotima] is not there. Socrates reports her views. Perhaps he distorts them unwittingly and unknowingly" (1992, 64 and 70). And later, Irigaray seems wary of Socrates' ability to accurately convey Diotima's conception of love when she states, "Carnal procreation is suspended in favor of the engendering of beautiful and good things. Immortal things. That, surprisingly, is the view of Diotima. At least as translated through the words uttered by Socrates" (73). Hence, Irigaray's use of "miscarries" (échoue) brings to mind the image of "Socrates as midwife"[11] and suggests that perhaps it is Socrates who does not properly deliver Diotima of her views.[12] Perhaps it is Socrates who has mis-carried her words. Diotima's method does not simply fail; rather, it is her mouthpiece, Socrates, who sends her method awry.

Whereas Diotima had given love the role of intermediary, her miscarriage, in Irigaray's view, is induced by the very introduction of the child. That is, Diotima's method miscarries at the very point at which Diotima "emphasizes the procreative aspect of love" (1992, 69). "Instead of allowing the child to germinate or develop in the milieu of love and fecundity between man and woman," Irigaray says, "[Diotima] seeks a cause of love in the animal world: procreation" (70). The consequence of "her" emphasis on procreation, over a "fecundity in itself," is that:

> The intermediary becomes the child, and no longer love. Occupy-
> ing the place of love, the child can no longer be a lover. It is put
> in the place of the incessant movement of love. (70)

Whereas Diotima had held that love is neither lover nor beloved, but both, in the movement from intermediary to telos, love gets "trapped in the beloved" (70). "A beloved who is an end is substituted for love between man and woman" (70). The movement in-between bodies is suspended. Although Diotima had first proposed love as a third term between lovers, "In the second part of her speech, she used love itself as a *means*. She cancelled out its intermediary function and subjected it to a telos" (76). Irigaray maintains, "A sort of teleological triangle replaces a perpetual movement, a perpetual transvaluation, a permanent becoming" (70). Thus, with the onset of Diotima's miscarriage, love is no longer ambiguous; rather, it is essentially defined. "Love," Irigaray says, "founds a family" (73). Women become significant only insofar as they provide for men.

According to Irigaray, the move toward a telos—a move that undermines love's position as intermediary—suggests that the view of love presented here is, as Kuykendall states, "deeply masculinist" (1992, 62). Although "Diotima" had reconceived love in the first part of her speech—and subsequently entered men and women into a "new" relation—in the second part of the speech, she goes on to adopt the sort of teleological view of love that she had initially rejected. Not only had Diotima rejected such a view, she had had to persuade Socrates against it. Such persuasion is of the type Irigaray notes when she says, "[E]ach time that Socrates thinks he can take some-thing as certain, [Diotima] undoes his certainty" (1992, 65–66). "She con-tinuously undoes his work . . . creating there some interval, play, something in motion and unlimited which disturbs his perspective" (Irigaray 1993a, 10). At these moments of undoing, which culminate in Diotima's miscar-riage, it is as if Socrates, who had attempted to speak the views of a woman, had nonetheless revealed himself as a man. Socrates' male body seeps through to permeate the discourse. The significance of the body emerges to materi-alize the message. Let me make this point in terms of the issue of sexual difference: whereas sexual difference had been revealed in Diotima's recon-ception of the relation between men and women, the issue is then covered over by Socrates' perhaps "unwitting distortion," perhaps "man-handling," of that very conception. It is in this respect that Socrates can be said to have caused the miscarriage of Diotima's reconception.

To say that Socrates is the cause of Diotima's miscarriage is to say, as Barbara Freeman points out, that the conception of love as "being subject to a telos," is essentially a masculine formulation of love (1988, 165). This formulation is attached to a male morphology, through which desire (not only for men, but in general) has come to be defined in terms of a cessation of tension (that is, ejaculation) (165). Freeman explains:

> [Platonic] desire constitutes itself as a lack to be filled and hence, abolished. Desire, thus, should be extinguished as quickly as pos-sible—sublated and sublimated—so that the integrity of bodily form can be restored and the body can return to its "normal" state. (169)

As opposed to a moment of tension, Irigaray states that "desire ought to be thought of as a changing dynamic . . . never definitely predicted" (1993a, 8). "Giving it a permanent definition would amount to suppressing it as desire" (8). In relation to a masculine conception of desire, women have come to be quite literally defined as "lacks to be filled." "He contains or envelops her with walls while enveloping himself and his things with her flesh" (Irigaray 1993a, 11). "*Woman*," Freeman maintains, "has been defined only as the sex which lacks what man has. The feminine has simply meant man's inverse or opposite; and woman, as the possibility of a genuine sexual difference rather than one term in a binarism, does not exist in Western thought" (166–67).[13] Irigaray alludes to the rendering of men and women in terms of binaries (for example, active/passive, physical/spiritual, time/space, lover/beloved, etc.) in asking of Diotima's miscarriage, "Is this the founding act of the metaphysi-cal?" (1992, 70). The perpetual passage between terms has been replaced, Irigaray suggests, by an ontology of separation.[14]

At the beginning of her essay, Irigaray reminds her readers that "Diotima is not invited to eat or to teach. And Diotima is not the only example of a woman whose wisdom, above all in love, is reported in her absence by a man" (1992, 64). Thus, the question of a masculine presence and a feminine absence underlies the motivation of Irigaray's reading of Diotima's discourse. Of central importance to Irigaray's reading is the fact that Diotima's views on love are placed in the mouth of a man (they are in this limited sense "present"), while Diotima herself—and all other women—are "absent." Perhaps it is in keeping with her role as intermediary that Diotima lingers in-between presence and absence in this way. Diotima resides in-between male and female bodies and positions. All the same, as Kuykendall states, "The fact that a male philosopher is speaking for an absent woman, a fact that is supposed to be irrelevant to the explicit celebration of love as universal, renders that celebration ironic" (1992, 62). And as Freeman states, "The flute-girl's absence marks and can even be seen to occasion the dialogue proper" (1988, 168).

Interestingly, the puzzle standardly associated with Diotima's discourse, as Andrea Nye articulates, is this: "How can the great Socrates, founder of philosophy, be saying that he learned everything he knows from a woman?" (1992, 78). To this question, Nye herself responds by saying that the puzzle dissolves if Diotima is viewed as an actual historical figure and is given her due authority by considering the historical circumstances of the time. However, it is not in response to this question that Irigaray provides *her* reading. Rather, Irigaray's reading calls into question the very prominence of this question itself. As Diotima "teaches [Socrates] the renunciation of already established truths" (Irigaray 1992, 65), Irigaray turns the standard question on its head. Irigaray does not ask how Socrates can claim to learn everything he knows from a woman; rather, she implicitly asks how it is that the view of Diotima can be adequately conveyed by a man. Moreover, it is precisely the tendency to interpret Diotima as a Platonist that Irigaray is concerned to call into question. For Irigaray, it is important not only to note that the conception of love presented in the *Symposium* is masculinist, it is likewise and perhaps more important to consider why the Platonic interpretation of Diotima's discourse is so pervasive. Ultimately, in Irigaray's view, the Platonic interpretation of Diotima persists because, as she states, "[m]an has been the subject of discourse, whether in theory, morality, and politics. And the gender of God, the guardian of every subject and every discourse, is always masculine and paternal" (1993a, 6–7). Minimally, the dialogue—written by a man—is then translated and commented upon by men.

Thus, we cannot accurately say that "Diotimean love is the same for all, women and men, and makes no distinction between feminine and masculine," and therefore, that the discourse of Diotima is put into masculine form because it is only men who are being addressed on the particular occasion of the *Symposium* (Nye 1992, 68). This sort of response precisely invites at least one question implicit in Irigaray's account; that is, "Why *are* only men present?" Although the conception of love is being claimed as universal, it is neither put into universal language nor is it directed at a universal audience. It is thereby this very pretension to universality that must be rendered suspicious.

In her opening essay of *An Ethics of Sexual Difference*, Irigaray states:

> We need to reinterpret everything concerning the relations between the subject and discourse. Everything, beginning with the way in which the subject has always been written in the masculine form, as *man*, even when it claimed to be universal or neutral. Despite the fact that man—at least in French—rather than being neutral is sexed. (1993a, 6)[15]

Keeping with this claim, Freeman maintains that "Irigaray's initiative [is] to allege that the West's definition of desire, despite its pretension to be gender-free might after all be thoroughly male" (1988, 169). As a consequence, Freeman continues:

> When the philosophy of erotic love is formulated, as in the *Symposium*, one cannot assume that woman is included in or that the discourse is addressed to or is necessarily true for women. (167)

The *Symposium* can therefore be taken as an instance of, or a dramatization of, Irigaray's broader claim with respect to sexual difference. Although the question of sexual difference is not explicitly posed in Diotima's discourse in the *Symposium*—the dialogue, in fact, exemplifies the fact that the question of sexual difference has not been traditionally posed—Diotima's reconception of love as intermediate between pairs of opposites nonetheless serves to foster between men and women a "new" relation (one in which love is not subjected to a masculine telos). Love is placed in-between male and female bodies. In this respect, Diotima's discourse exposes, to a limited extent, the very issue of sexual difference. However, the issue of sexual difference is again covered over; for Diotima, this is the occasion for, and the result of, her miscarriage.

Concerning the movement from intermediary to telos, and its relation to *eros*, Irigaray remarks:

> If the couple of lovers cannot care for the place of love like a third term between them, then they will not remain lovers and cannot give birth to lovers. Something gets solidified in space-time with the loss of a vital intermediary milieu of an accessible, loving, transcendental. (1992, 70)

With the solidification (or freezing) of space-time, the two sexes are separated into opposing binaries. The preservation and mediation of their difference disappears; the reconceived relation between men and women "risks being replaced by a meta-physics" (Irigaray 1992, 76). Thus, Irigaray's concern with sexual difference and her related interest in "reconsidering the whole problematic of space and time" (1993a, 7) informs her reading of the discourse of Diotima. For Irigaray, Diotima precisely presents—and herself represents—such a (re)conception of space-time. As Irigaray concludes, "[Angels] speak like messengers, but gesture seems to be their 'nature' " (16).

IRIGARAY'S (RE)FIGURING OF PLACE

Along with rethinking our relation to space and time, Irigaray maintains that to think through the issue of sexual difference requires a change in our conception of "the *inhabiting of places,* and of *containers,* or *envelopes of identity*" (1993a, 7). Irigaray states, "We must reconsider the whole question of our conception of place in order to move on to another age of difference" (11–12). Whereas in the myth of Aristophanes in Plato's *Symposium*—the story to which Irigaray returns in the final pages of her essay on Aristotle—the original whole creature was first embraced in movement, when Zeus splits the creature in two and then allows it to reunite through love, Irigaray claims, "[t]he yoking of two into one same one paralyzes the whole scene. There is no space between him and her, between the men and the women" (1993b, 46). Although the speech of Aristophanes interestingly accounts for the existence of the navel,[16] this "most irreducible mark of birth" is nonetheless concealed by, or rendered into, a male (godly) creation (cf. Irigaray 1993b, v, 14 and 16).[17] The site of original connection with the mother, the womb, is forgotten.

Irigaray indicates that Aristotle, in his treatise on place in *Physics* IV, does not mention the womb or the relationship between mother and child. Aristotle neglects the mother-child relation—the relation between these two bodies—despite the fact that he investigates the issue of containers and their connection with what they contain. Aristotle asks in chapter I, for example, "What shall we say about *growing* things?," but he does not mention the child (or the fetus); and he states in chapter II, "Place is supposed to be something like a vessel—the vessel being a transportable place,"[18] but he does not point to the mother (or the womb) as the primal vessel. Irigaray remarks, "The maternal-feminine remains the place separated from 'its' own place, deprived of 'its' place. She is or ceaselessly becomes the place of the other who cannot separate himself from it" (1993a, 10). While the question of sexual difference—like that of women or bodies—has been denied a place, the issue of sexual difference is nevertheless unveiled for Irigaray within Aristotle's treatise on place. As the issue of sexual difference resists erasure within the discourse of Diotima, sexual difference likewise discloses itself in Aristotle's *Physics* IV. As sexual difference is both concealed and revealed in Plato's *Symposium*, so too is that movement encountered within Aristotle's examination of place.[19]

While Irigaray asks of Diotima's "miscarriage," "Is this the founding act of the meta-physical?" (1992, 70), regarding Aristotle's treatise on place, Irigaray remarks, "The *relationship between envelope and things* constitutes one of the aporias, or the aporia, of Aristotelianism and of the philosophical systems derived from it" (1993a, 10). As the mis-carriage of Diotima's views indicates the division of reality into opposing binaries, Irigaray's focus on Aristotle's *Physics* suggests that it marks yet another founding moment in the history of Western metaphysics and its elision of sexual difference.

The Womb as Figure of Sexual Difference

When Irigaray reopens "the figures of philosophical discourse" (1985b, 74–75), she highlights "figures" in more than one sense. Her task can be considered an "excavation"—an uncovering of texts of central philosophical figures (for example, Plato and Aristotle), of specific mythological figures in some of these texts (for example, Diotima and Antigone), as well as of figures, in the sense of "matrixes" or "frameworks," in which the feminine is presumably contained but of which the feminine nonetheless threatens to disrupt. Irigaray states, "The womb, for its part, would figure rather as place. Though of course what unfolds in the womb unfolds in function of an interval, a cord, that is never done away with" (1993a, 49). "The interval cannot be done away with" (Irigaray 1993a, 49).

Although Irigaray returns to a notion of the interval, her intention is not to recover it in its traditional meaning. Rather, Irigaray desires, in a sense, to refigure the interval. She seeks to open the interval, to uncover what has been suppressed or "repressed." Similarly, although Irigaray gestures toward the womb, her aim is not to return women to their traditional role as mothers. Irigaray neither envisions women as *mere* containers nor essentializes women by attaching "the feminine" necessarily to an anatomical/physiological part of women's bodies; namely, the womb. Instead, Irigaray sees in the womb, or the maternal-feminine, the possibility of an unthought relation (cf. Irigaray 1993a, 5).

While women have been traditionally rendered the passive objects or "places" of attraction, men have actively moved toward them (Irigaray 1993a, 9). In this movement, men have risked, or feared, absorption/consumption (that is, castration). Irigaray states:

> Once there was the enveloping body and the enveloped body, the latter being more mobile through what Aristotle termed *locomotion* (since maternity doesn't look much like "motion"). The one who offers or allows desire moves and envelopes, engulfing the other. (12)

Irigaray proposes that "beginning with those [philosophers] whose names define some age in the history of philosophy, we have to point out how the break with material contiguity is made, how the system is put together, how the specular economy works" (1985b, 75). She thereby points to Aristotle as marking a definitive moment within the tradition of Western metaphysics. Thus, if Diotima's discourse reveals an innovative relation between pairs of oppositions (for example, men and women, and time and space), then the word *intervalle* is likewise significant since *intervalle* is not exclusively defined in terms of time or space. Instead, *intervalle* is both temporal and spatial in meaning—having senses of "in time" and "space between" (cf. Butler 1993, 252 n 16). "*Between*," Irigaray states, "in the interval of time, of times. Weaving the veil of time, time with space, time in space" (1993a, 53). Importantly, for Aristotle, "space is empty" and "time is linked to motion" (Grosz 1994, 93). Hence, there is an alignment, in the work of Aristotle, of women with space and men with time. And there is a priority granted, given Aristotle's overall emphasis on motion, to the temporal (male) over the spatial (female).

At the beginning of his treatise on place, Aristotle suggests, "we must find in how many ways one thing is said to be *in* another" (210a 14). The "most basic way of all" is for a thing to be "in a vessel and, generally, in a place" (Aristotle 210a 23–24). Place is most essentially a "surrounder" (Aristotle 209b 31–33). Regarding Aristotle's response of "surrounder," Edward Hussey remarks:

> A vessel surrounds what is in it; but it may also be said to "receive" or be occupied by what is in it. . . . Aristotle does not here distinguish the "receptive" from the "circumscriptive" aspects of being in a vessel or a place. (1983, 108)

While women have been conceived as envelopes or containers for men, women's acts of receiving men have been neutralized. Women have been rendered passive/static spaces instead of active/dynamic sites. Defining "place," Aristotle claims, "The place of a thing is the innermost motionless boundary of what contains it" (212a 20–21).[20] "Controlling, comprising, composing," Hussey states, "may all be thought of as analogous to surrounding" (1983, 109). Whereas men have been granted mobility (locomotion, activity), women have been rendered immobile (motionless, passive). Hence, Irigaray asks, "Hasn't woman been imagined as passive only because man would fear to lose mastery in that particular act?" (1993a, 44).

As opposed to a passive container, Irigaray indicates, "[Woman] gives form to the male sex (organ) and sculpts it from within. She becomes the container and the active *place* of the sexual act" (1993a, 43). "Woman, insofar as she is a container," Irigaray states, "is never a closed one. Place is never closed. The boundaries touch against one another while still remaining open" (51). For Irigaray, the sexual act has always been conceived on the basis of a reproductive model. Maternity has been "eternally confused with the sexuation of the female body" (Irigaray 1993a, 43). Hence men, in the sexual act, strive toward the womb—which, as Irigaray notes, they can never reach. At the same time, men ignore the skin of women as containing—as holding—them. Men ignore the material, bodily sites of women. Irigaray maintains that the sexed female body "would not have to be especially passive" (Irigaray 1993a, 43). Rather, femininity/women have been relegated or necessitated, by men, as passive.

Within a discussion of Irigaray's figure of the maternal-feminine, Tina Chanter suggests that "[b]y naming together—as if they were inseparable—the maternal and the feminine, Irigaray indicates the traditional understanding of women as mothers. One of her tasks then is to make such a differentiation possible" (1995, 16). For Irigaray, women must be differentiated both as desiring subjects and as maternal figures. Irigaray states that no thought has been given to what takes place within women themselves. No consideration has been granted to what unfolds within the womb, within the vessel, that "woman contains invisibly" (Irigaray 1993a, 53). "Place, in her, is in place," Irigaray says, "not only as organs but as vessel or receptacle. It is place twice over: as mother and as woman" (52). Irigaray highlights the fact that women's sex has been thought in the singular—as reproductive organ/thing, as biological/functional matter—and never as vessel. "It seems as though she can be a container for only one thing," Irigaray says, "if that is her function" (41); but for child and for man, "she is not the same 'vessel' " (41). The relationship between bodies—women and children, women and men—is not a symmetrical relation.

Regarding the vessel, Martin Heidegger has indicated, in a very different context:

> We paid no heed to that in the vessel which does the containing.
> We have given no thought to how the containing itself goes on. It
> holds by keeping and retaining what it took in. The void holds in
> a twofold manner: taking and keeping. The word "hold" is therefore
> ambiguous. (1971, 171)

As the navel is *both* site of original connection with the mother *and* of separation from her, the womb (as vessel) is not a mere passive receptacle or space. The womb, rather, is an active place of formation, of nourishment, of "holding." The cord that unfolds within the womb serves both to connect two bodies and to maintain their separation. The umbilical cord, as interval between mother and child/fetus, allows a relation that is both "fitting and separate." It serves as a link in-between bodies. Precisely in virtue of its holding, its keeping and retaining, the womb has been neglected as a genuine container. While women have been presumed to be mere locations, Irigaray indicates, their very "status as envelope and thing(s) has not been interpreted" (1993a, 10).[21]

The Aporia *of "Place"*

In her reading of Aristotle, Irigaray draws a parallel between the issue of place and that of sexual difference (cf. 1993a, 39). Offering reasons to investigate place, Aristotle writes, "All suppose that things which exist are somewhere and . . . motion in its most general and proper sense is change in place, which we call 'locomotion' " (208a 29–32). According to Hussey:

> The primary purpose of Aristotle's discussion of place is to make locations respectable; that is, to give an account, compatible with Aristotelian physics and metaphysics, of how there can be such things as locations which persist at least for a time and are for that time in existence independently of any body which happens to be located in them. (1983, xxvii)

Aristotle has "a half-declared metaphysical interest. He is inquiring into how we can plausibly turn locations into features of the world that are 'semi-permanent' and 'semi-independent' " (Hussey 1983, xxviii). In formulating the problem of locations or of place in this way, Aristotle precisely, though unwittingly, states the problem of sexual difference. That is, women have never been allowed an independent existence; rather, women have always—and only—existed in relation to men's definitions. Women have been defined by what they passively contain: men's penises, children/fetuses. "As for woman," Irigaray says, "she is place" (1993a, 35). Women are not simply one more place among others; they are, perhaps, place itself.

Stating the common view of place, Aristotle indicates that "[t]he existence of place is held to be obvious from the fact of mutual replacement. Where water now is . . . when the water has gone out as from a vessel, air is present; and at another time another body occupies this same place" (208b 1–4). It is, perhaps, due to the presumed *obvious* nature of place that—as Aristotle notes—"we have inherited nothing from previous thinkers" (208a 34–35). As Irigaray maintains, again drawing a parallel between place and sexual difference, place has been ignored or excluded from consideration both prior and subsequent to Aristotle. Place, like sexual difference, has been assumed to be simply apparent, evident, and clear.

On the issue of place, Aristotle is puzzled because, for one thing, place is strictly neither form nor matter. Place is [at] neither pole of the form/matter binary. Aristotle states, "Insofar as it is separable from the thing it is not the form, and insofar as it contains it, it is different from the matter" (209b 30–32). And later Aristotle claims, "Since the vessel is nothing pertaining to that which is in it . . . place will not be either the matter or the form, but something else" (210b 27–31). Being neither form nor matter, the place of place is unclear. Place cannot be aligned, simply, with either term of a binarism. Separate (from the thing), but containing (the thing)—this, for Aristotle, is the puzzle of place. While Aristotle wishes to account for place within his system, place acts to disrupt—or to confound—his framework. Hussey explains:

> It is natural to think of the place of a three-dimensional body as being itself three-dimensional. But then a place ought itself to be a body, since an Aristotelian characterization of a body is "what is extended in three dimensions" (e.g., *de Caelo* I.1, 268a). In that case, a body's occupying a place would constitute a coincidence of two distinct bodies—assuming that the place of a body is not identical with the body. But two distinct bodies cannot coincide. (1983, 102; Aristotle 209a 4–7)

With the claim that "two distinct bodies cannot coincide," Aristotle makes the point, in a sense contra egalitarian feminism, that two bodies cannot assume the same place. In terms of sex and gender, this is to say that two sexes can never be identical with respect to gender (cf. Gatens 1991). However, in claiming their lack of coincidence, Aristotle separates the distinct bodies (the sexes)—giving each a separate, "natural," teleological place. Thus, Aristotle blocks a genuine relation between them. There is no connection in-between bodies. Or, perhaps it could be said that the bodies are not allowed to coincide precisely because they are first conceived as distinct (that is, mutually exclusive). Moreover, on Irigaray's reading, Aristotle precisely ignores the coincidence of women's bodies with the bodies of children, or of men, that they sometimes contain.[22]

For Irigaray, it is Aristotle's puzzle with respect to place that offers the possibility of a genuine alliance or relation. "Fitting and separate," Irigaray asks, "—is this the horizon of the meeting of the sexes in its different dimensions? With reversals of envelopes and envelopings" (1993a, 47). Hence, rather than resolve the difficulties of place within Aristotle's existing framework, Irigaray claims, "We need to change the relations between form, matter, interval, and limit, an issue that has never been considered in a way that allows for a relationship between two loving subjects of different sexes" (1993a, 11). "We must constitute a possible place for each sex, body, and flesh to inhabit" (Irigaray 1993a, 17–18).

By emphasizing generation, Aristotle renders impossible, in Irigaray's view, a genuine meeting between men and women. Demarcating the boundary between the sexes via the telos of desire destroys the possibility of an alliance or encounter (a "co-location") of two distinct bodies. Aristotle aligns men with form and women with matter from the outset by anchoring their point of connection in reproduction.[23] As a consequence, the sexes are both separated and fused: men and women stand in fundamental opposition to one another, while one sex is ultimately absorbed by the other. Form, for instance, is always already prioritized over matter. Moreover, as Jonathan

Lear points out, "form exists not merely as a realized state, it also exists as a *striving* toward that state. It is an irreducible force . . . directed toward an end" (1988, 35). As the second part of Diotima's speech exposes an underlying masculine conception of desire, the striving for form—the directedness toward an end or a product—demonstrates, on Irigaray's account, a masculine formulation of desire within Aristotle's discussion of place. For Aristotle, the "overcoming of the interval" marks "the cause of locomotion" (Irigaray 1993a, 48), whereas for Irigaray, "If desire is to subsist, a double place is necessary, a double envelope. . . . In this sense, the interval would produce place" (48).

Despite Aristotle's apparent place for women (as providers of matter in generation, whereby they presumably assume a place within the form/matter binary), rather than being contained within that pairing, women disrupt or are displaced by the oppositions of form and matter. "Woman," Irigaray says, "is assigned to be place without occupying a place" (1993a, 52). "She gave place yet has no place, except her womb and even then . . ." (Irigaray 1993b, 33). Defined in terms of Aristotelian matter, women are subordinated to men/form from the outset, while women as "place as such" are paradoxical to the very system. Aristotle's system—his categories—does not account for place. Like Freud's "riddle of the nature of femininity," or Hegel's rendering womankind "ironic," the fact that place confounds his framework is cause for Aristotle to ask of women—under the veil of "place"—"What in the world . . . are we to suppose place to be?" (209a, 14).[24]

While Aristotle's treatise on place precisely excludes women from thematization, the Aristotelian rendering of containers as limiting and controlling displays men's anxieties over castration. Irigaray states, "She is merely a receptacle whose dimensions must be determined in case they prove threatening" (1985a, 166). Forgotten in the notion of a container or vessel as a limit to what it holds is its "function" to receive and embrace what it takes in; that is, the *ambiguity* involved in "holding." The vessel does not solely confine what it holds, it likewise nurtures it. Moreover, a traditional container is only considered capable of containing one thing at a time (cf. Aristotle 1987, 208b 1–4). As containers, on the traditional rendering, women can be the place for either men's penises or children/fetuses. While men's anxieties of being "consumed" in the sexual act are fears of being absorbed into the womb, these fears are nonetheless "mis-placed" ones. Anxiety over castration confuses one place (the sexual organ) for another (the reproductive one), while simultaneously rendering both—already collapsed into one—as limiting and confining.

The idea that women surround men in the sexual act reintroduces Irigaray's claim that the sexes must enjoy a relation of *mutual* enveloping. There must be a rethought relation in-between these bodies. Central to this claim is the meaning of "to envelope" or "to hold." Traditionally, such holding has been rendered passive, and the passivity of the vessel has linked women to their traditional place as receptacles—mere empty spaces or "voids." In opposition to the presumed emptiness in/of women, men have been considered "ill-equipped" to (mutually) hold. In their activity, men have been granted a different function. Irigaray points out the forgotten active role of the container. The vessel is not properly a mere passive space; it is, rather, an active site or "holder."

Insofar as Irigaray opposes an androgynous or symmetrical relation between the sexes, if men are to be place for women at all, they cannot do so in the same way as women are place for men.[25] That is, whereas a forgotten element of activity must accompany women in their reconceived role of container, a certain feature of passivity must accompany men in their ability to contain. Any activity of female bodies serving as containers is not equivalent to any passivity of male bodies serving the same function. This is to reiterate Gatens's point that the activity (read "masculinity") of female bodies differs in meaning from that of male bodies, and the passivity (read "femininity") of male bodies differs in meaning from that of female bodies.

For Irigaray, the relation between mother and child within the womb serves as a model or figure for a genuine thinking of sexual difference. The relation between mother and child is neither a relation of part (child) to whole (mother), nor one of two independent wholes. Instead, the relation between mother and child is—in virtue of the umbilical cord—one of both connection and separation between two bodies. Although the cord mediating in-between two bodies can be physically cut at birth, Irigaray suggests that the interval in-between bodies (the relation of both dependence and independence) cannot be done away with. Irigaray asks:

> Does the father replace the womb with the matrix of his language? The family name . . . always stands at one remove from that most elemental identity tag: the scar where the umbilical cord was cut. The family name, and even the first name, slip over the body like clothes, like identity tags— outside the body. (1993b, 14)

Before the mark of language, the first relation takes the "form" of an exchange in-between bodies. Despite efforts to transcend the material/body, the scar of the navel nonetheless resists a complete "forgetting." As a scar, the navel is ambiguous between a wound and a site of healing. It is not that the navel's existence merely fades from awareness, it is more accurately the case that the navel itself is concealed by "clothes." Thus, in Irigaray's view, "mother-matter" cannot be interpreted as innocently missing from Aristotle's treatise on place. Instead, his neglect represents a movement or a turning away from the first and paradigmatic place. As Irigaray herself concludes, "She gave place yet she has no place, even then. . . ." (1993b, 33).[26]

CHAPTER THREE

CONTINGENCY AND RACE

—————————————————————————

White is what a woman is; not white is what she had better not be.

—Hammonds 1999

My old man died in a fine big house. My ma died in a shack. I wonder where I'm gonna die, Being neither white nor black?

—Hughes 1986

SEXUAL DIFFERENCE, RACE, BODIES

Given Irigaray's concern with sexual difference as an *ontological* category, it is necessary to address charges that sexual difference theories—and Irigaray's work in particular—have neglected consideration of race. Charges against Irigaray maintain that she affords sexual difference a privilege that effectively relegates race to a secondary status. In turn, to position race as secondary in relation to sexual difference is not only to conceive of "race" as a subordinated category, it is likewise to render race invisible within a framework informed by sexual difference. Given the precise desire of sexual difference theorists to dismantle dualistic structures, to appropriate and reiterate them (by way of a sex/race binary) is especially problematic for this theoretical work itself.

Perhaps more importantly, to claim an ontological status for sexual difference is to construct sexual difference as unmarked by race. However, it is not possible to be unmarked (or neutral) with respect to race—especially when considering lived bodies. Rather, to formulate sexual difference as more primary than matters of race likely harbors a white notion of sexual difference. Thus, instead of representing an unmarked or neutral category, sexual difference is more plausibly marked as white. Marjorie Hass has suggested that "race remains invisible in both Irigaray's theoretical and empirical work" (2000, 84).

45

Theoretically, for Hass, "Irigaray's analytic methods encourage identification of the similarities rather than the differences between [women]" (84). However, when considered as an empirical issue, Hass contends, "the primacy of sex" may "point to an incompleteness in Irigaray's research . . . that could be rectified by adapting Irigaray's methodology to this site of analysis" (84)—"the site of analysis" referring to matters of race. For Chanter, the issue of Irigaray's neglect of race is problematic in that it takes sexual difference "as foundational," deriving other differences from it and continuing "to privilege whiteness" (forthcoming, 20). Nonetheless, Chanter continues, "Where Irigaray's analysis remains powerful, even indispensable, is in its identification of the immense difficulty we have, both as theorists and practitioners, in resisting the monological impulse that reduces all difference to the same" (20).

While I agree with the lines of critique offered by both Hass and Chanter, my concern here is not so much with whether Irigaray's methodology could be extended to consider race even though Irigaray herself neglects matters of race. Rather, my aim is to decenter Irigaray altogether, foregrounding instead writing by several theorists who precisely do address race. In particular, I am interested in discussions of race that conceptualize the category in a manner suggestive of the contingency relation explicated in chapter 1. That is to say, I wish to examine and center work in race theory, reflecting back on sexual difference theory (and not the reverse). This approach is informed by the conviction that even if Irigaray's methodology could be extended to matters of race, to position Irigaray's work as a model for such an analysis would still act to subordinate race theorists to Irigaray's example. Rather, I wish to draw connections to sexual difference theory from the position of race theory, more centrally focusing on Gatens's notion of contingency than on Irigaray's discussion of sexual difference. More precisely, I wish to highlight writing by race theorists that considers race in a way compatible with Gatens's account of the relationship between sex and gender. On these accounts, "race" is posited as existing in-between construction and constraint, as never fully fabricated nor granted. In this regard, the examples referred to below offer a way of conceiving race that keeps with Gatens's construal of contingency. To conceive of race as a contingent category acts to position it in-between essentialist and constructionist conceptions. In turn, this positioning arguably affords a more accurate account and understanding of lived experience.

In what follows, I primarily discuss race via the categories of *white* and *black*, and I follow the logic expressed by Lewis Gordon in *Bad Faith and Anti-Black Racism*. Gordon states:

Since the Western valuative system has historically placed positivity and its self-identity on the value of the white, that means that its primary opposition is structured on the level of the black. To speak of racial oppression, then, is to speak of the white and black. (1997, 122)

In highlighting the position of blackness within Western thought, Gordon emphasizes black bodies as assuming the paradigmatic place of "otherness" within these structures. Black bodies have been conceived in relation to white bodies, while white bodies have marked the racial standard. That is to say, Western frameworks have overwhelmingly conceived of the races as oppositionally ordered, mutually exclusive categories, while they have simultaneously positioned whiteness on the top of a hierarchical ordering. This positioning itself can be traced to a particular rendering of black and white bodies.

In his essay, "Black Bodies, White Bodies," Sander L. Gilman addresses nineteenth-century medical discourse in which the sexual organs of black female bodies are described as "much more developed than those of white [bodies]" (1985, 232).[1] The so-called "overdevelopment" of black female genitalia, and the protrusion of black female buttocks, is then linked to the alleged primitiveness of black women in general. The paradigmatic case of "the black woman" is the Hottentot, whose sexual parts are depicted as looking different, being anomalous, and appearing hideous in form (Gilman 1985, 232). Through this transfer (from bodily appearance to group quality), a particular bodily interpretation (vis-à-vis sex) acts to embody specific characteristics (vis-à-vis gender).

However, the image of the Hottentot not only signaled beliefs about black *women* in general; rather, the image was extended to represent blacks as a class. Blacks, by way of the Hottentot, were thought to assume a primitive nature. The primitiveness of the black was likewise positioned in opposition to the civility of the white. Gilman remarks:

> The antithesis of European sexual mores and beauty is embodied in the black, and the essential black is the Hottentot. The physical appearance of the Hottentot is, indeed, the central nineteenth century icon for sexual difference between the European and the black. (1985, 231)

Thus, the conceived primitive nature of blacks, in relation to whites, has been grounded in black bodies—bodies considered more (sexually) developed than those of their white referent. In the words of Gilman, a medical model placed "both the sexuality and the beauty of the black in an antithetical position to that of the white" and based this judgment on observable physical differences between the black and the European (1985, 231). The figure of the black woman was central to this medicalized conception of the raced body,[2] serving to symbolize a purported difference between the races.

In essence, racial difference was conceived in sexual(ized) ways, thereby crossing race with sexuality (and sexual difference). Exaggerated features of black bodies were thought to imply a heightened sexuality and, by extension, a primitive character.

Interestingly, underlying the view of blacks as primitive in relation to whites is a conception of black bodies as overdeveloped in relation to (white) European ones. That is, lack of complexity in blacks, rather than being attributed to underdevelopment, is precisely ascribed to the reverse. We might recall Laqueur, here, and the idea that there is no bodily fact of the matter. Instead, bodies are always already subject to interpretation. Thus, through the interpretation of bodies presented in nineteenth-century medical discourse, the physical (the biological, "black body") and the mental (a notion of "black culture") are linked by presumed necessity.[3] This conflation, also recognized as a form of scientific racism, implies that blacks, as James Davis notes, "are believed to share certain values and patterns of behavior, because it is just 'in their blood'" (1993, 24). Given this context, reference to "racial difference" has been considered suspect due to its typically negative construction. At times, blacks have themselves averted racial difference and avoided the body, since adopting a stance of difference has meant assuming the dominant discourse placing blacks in a position of inferiority. Hence, at the end of the nineteenth century, in 1897, W. E. B. DuBois attempted to garner support for a more positive construal of racial difference. In "The Conservation of Races," DuBois remarked:

> The American Negro [has attempted to] "minimize race distinctions" [through] the denial of difference [because] back of most of the discussions of race with which he is familiar, have lurked certain assumptions as to his natural abilities, as to his political, intellectual and moral status, which he felt were wrong. (in Appiah 1985, 25)

While DuBois aimed to unhinge racial difference from negative assumptions, he did not seek to deny difference in matters of race. Rather, he posited a unique contribution to be made by the Negro race to humanity. In this way, DuBois maintained difference, while he offered a space to rethink and reconceive what that difference might mean.

Necessity and Arbitrariness

If the connection between bodies and cultures is taken to be one of necessity, as with the nineteenth-century medicalized conception of race, then raced cultures absorb racially marked bodies. That is, notions of white culture or black culture are seen as the necessary outgrowths of white bodies or black bodies respectively. Within the traditional framework, black cultures/ black bodies and white cultures/white bodies are conceived as necessary units.

To say that bodies are absorbed by cultures means that cultures assume focus over bodies and the significance of bodies is forgotten. This view results in what can be described as the essentialist belief that black folks (or white folks) just *are* a certain way. While an interpretation of bodies underscores this view, the interpretative nature of it is precisely forgotten in its perpetuation. For instance, the idea that race is not a natural, genetic, and static category has only recently been challenged.

However, if to escape an alleged necessary connection between black bodies and black cultures (or white bodies and white cultures)[4] one claims that the relationship between the two terms is not necessary, but is instead arbitrary, then we arrive at a similar problem to that discussed in chapter 1. To take the relation between cultures and bodies as merely arbitrary means that cultures displace bodies. White and black cultures are believed capable of mapping onto either white or black bodies, with these mappings (white cultures/white bodies or white cultures/black bodies; black cultures/white bodies or black cultures/black bodies) presumably rendering the same meanings. In the first case, minds and bodies (or raced cultures/raced bodies) collapse; one term absorbs the other. In the second case, when the relation is conceived as merely arbitrary, the two terms radically separate—becoming detached and unconnected.

Consequently, to conceive the relationship between raced cultures and raced bodies as either necessary or arbitrary fails to sufficiently account for the body. In other words, the meaning attributed to bodies is not adequately incorporated into such a conception of race. On the issue of arbitrariness, Lucius Outlaw states, in *On Race and Philosophy*:

> I wish to argue against those who regard raciality and ethnicity (and gender) as nothing more than arbitrary, fluid, socially contestable "fictive," "imagined," or "ideological" "social constructions," that, according to some persons, are not even *real* even though real enough in what are regarded as their social or "material" effects. (1996, 8)

Here, Outlaw wishes to afford race a standing more substantial than that provided by formulations of race as a sheer construct. At the same time, such a reality granted to race is not intended to imply an essentialism or biological grounding.

Race Relations

Moreover, the assumption that particular cultures can be entirely separated from bodies is found in what bell hooks calls, "the liberal belief in a universal subjectivity (we are all just people)" (1992, 167). The liberal view implies that there is no distinct difference between whites and blacks—in essence, whites and blacks are ultimately the same. hooks names this view "the myth of sameness" or "the notion of racial erasure" (1992, 167 and 12). The liberal response to an idea of racial essence (black folks are a certain way) is to claim that we are all the same (humans are a certain way). However, with this movement, racial difference is erased in favor of an underlying human sameness and is collapsed into a "mutual humanity." It could be argued that the notion of racial erasure is problematic in its disregard for bodies and the practical import attached to them. The myth of sameness thereby offers— precisely—a false sense of equality or sameness. Hence, it can be asked whether liberal color blindness is but one more form of racist ideology[5] insofar as it maintains an unequal structure through declarations against the existence of racial inequality (where equality is conflated with sameness).

Further, evidence that the relation between raced cultures and raced bodies is not a necessary one can be drawn from whites who act or think "black," and blacks who act or think "white." In turn, evidence that the cultures/bodies relation is not merely arbitrary can be gained from societal demand that white/white and black/black mappings be maintained.[6] This normative component to race implies that it is not whiteness per se that is valorized in our culture, but the whiteness of "white" bodies.[7] That is, differ- ent meanings are attributed to whiteness mapped onto "white" bodies, and whiteness attached to "black" bodies, illustrating that it is not whiteness as such, but the relation between whiteness and "white" bodies that is central within the culture. Therefore, racially marked bodies (black or white) can- not be transcended in an effort to adopt white or black characteristics.

For this reason, it is problematic when a white South African (for example) attempts to claim the term *African American* upon residing in the United States, or when whites consume aspects of black culture in a way that avoids the burden of being black in the United States. Of the latter phenom- enon, Greg Tate comments:

> The Black body, and subsequently Black culture, has become the hungered-after taboo item . . . something to be possessed and something to be erased—an operation that explains [among other things] the American music industry's never-ending quest for a white artist who can competently perform a Black musical impersonation. (2003, 4)

In the situation presented by Tate, a sought-after black culture is mapped onto white bodies in ways that transform the former. In other words, in seeking to consume black culture, whites effectively devour it. We could say that there is no relation of symmetry between racially marked bodies and their perfor- mances. Of course, the very lack of equivalent mappings is also why Michael Jackson's process of "turning white" has been the source of such negative critical commentary. While in the case of Jackson, the negative critique has centered on bodily alterations rather than on musical impersonations, this circumstance does suggest that within a white supremacist structure, black bodies are supposed to remain "in their place." Black folks may fault Jackson for a considered attempt to assimilate or merge into whiteness, while white folks may discredit him for the presumption that he can buy that whiteness. Both types of criticism nonetheless indicate the importance attached to the relationship between body and culture in considerations of race.

Whether true of Jackson or not, if dark skin has been (at times) derided, even by some members of those groups possessing it, then the association of light skin with whiteness and the valuing of whiteness over blackness is evidenced in this derision. Light skin, in other words, has been valued because it represents whiteness. However, it is important to note that whiteness cannot simply be equated with light skin, since "white" bodies can be tanned—thus becoming darker. And this darkness (that is, the dark skin of "white" bodies) has been valued, in many contexts, in ways that the dark skin of "black" bodies has not. The conflicting valuation between darkness/ "white" bodies and darkness/ "black" bodies renders problematic any association of race solely with skin color. Rather, it demonstrates that the relation between body and color is the bearer of significance. After all, tanned "white" bodies can closely resemble—in color—those of light "black" bodies, yet the meanings of these respective bodies widely varies.

To emphasize that the relationship between categories is of significance to race also suggests that to be raced is neither given nor static. Rather, to be raced represents a particular way of living one's body in relation to culture. In the words of hooks, "race" is "a matter of 'becoming' as well as 'being'" (hooks 1992, 5). It could then be said that "white" bodies and "black" bodies, themselves in positions of becoming, both assume and resist strict definitions. Or, to phrase this point another way, it could be said that raced bodies are *both* produced *and* resistant to production. Hence, if whiteness and blackness are connected to bodies, while not simply being reducible to them, then the relationship between raced bodies and raced cultures is shown to be neither one of necessity nor of arbitrariness. Instead, the relation is one of contingency.

THE CONTINGENCY RELATION AND THE IN-BETWEEN

Within literary texts, a contingent relation with respect to race is often illustrated in the work of Toni Morrison and Nella Larsen, among others. For instance, the character of Jadine Child in Morrison's *Tar Baby* (1981), while acting to deny her lineage or connection to blackness, is nonetheless haunted by the very identity she seeks to escape. Remarking on Jadine, Karla Holloway indicates, "Instead of Jadine having an inherent sense of herself as a Black woman, she has chosen to dispossess herself" (1987,120). However, while the identity of "black woman" is not simply given to Jadine, neither is such an identity open to complete escape or erasure, which is to say that the connection between Jadine and "black woman" is not an arbitrary matter.

Rather, Jadine's race imposes itself on her, and she must actively resist—or more positively assume—its intrusion. "Jadine Child," by name, is ambiguously situated vis-à-vis her race. One can wonder of Jadine, "Whose 'child' is she?" (Holloway 1987, 119). The character of Clare in Larsen's *Passing* (1994), unlike Jadine, "truly desires 'blackness' " (hooks 1992, 9). As hooks relays, "Clare boldly declares that she would rather live for the rest of her life as a poor black woman in Harlem than as a rich white matron downtown" (7). Despite her desire for blackness, Clare is nonetheless moved to assume a white identity, since "she only sees blackness as a sign of victimization and powerlessness" (hooks 1992, 18). Internalizing a fear of blackness, Clare opts to pass as white. In turn, Clare is able to pass as white because she looks white; that is, minimally, she has light—not dark—skin. With respect to her passing, Clare's fear is in being found out, or in being seen, as black (especially by her white husband with whom she is most intimate). This fear of being discovered is possible given the conception of race afforded by the one-drop rule. With the one-drop rule, "One need not look black in order to be a black" (Davis 1993, 125). Consequently, to be black contains a certain element of hiddenness (cf. Davis 1993, 143).

This state of affairs also explains why, historically, "[a]spiring pass-whites must not only look white but also prove that they are accepted as such in both informal and more institutional situations" (Davis 1993, 97). As Davis points out, "Appropriate class behavior must be demonstrated so that it is clear that the person 'acts white'" (1993, 97). This point can be rephrased to state that it is the perceived relation between light skin (or a particular bodily appearance) and certain classed behaviors that presumably renders the "look of whiteness."[8] To return for a moment to the Hottentot image, it is also significant to note that this figure not only represented a racialized icon via the interpretation of certain "raced" features, but the Hottentot icon itself was precisely racialized through its association with the lower class of the prostitute. The "disease" of the prostitute, and by extension black women (through the Hottentot) and blacks as a class (through black women), was set in opposition to the "purity" of white women and the white race.

In this regard, Hammonds reminds us that "[w]hite women were characterized as pure, passionless, and de-sexed, while black women were the epitome of immorality, pathology, impurity, and sex itself" (1999, 96). Hammonds adds that "the image of the black woman constructed in [the late nineteenth century] reflected everything the white woman was not" (95). This interpretive difference, grounded in an interpretation of white and black female bodies, additionally highlights the danger of monolithically referencing the category *woman*. In other words, not only have women been set in opposition to men, but women have been established as binaries between/ among themselves. While white women have been conceived as the "lack" of white men, black women have been rendered the "deviation" of white women. In this way, blackness has been maintained as measured against whiteness. Within this framework, the presumed significance and value of white is left intact. Consequently, for theorists such as hooks, to (re)think blackness—or to learn to adopt a stance that affirms blackness—means not only to reconsider blackness, it also means to interrogate the category of whiteness (cf. hooks 1992, 12).

It is also relevant that, in the historical case of passing, light-skinned blacks have often been degraded by other blacks aware of the passing. Having light skin, that is, must be combined with a black identification in order for a passing individual to be valued by the broader group. That is to say, light-skinned blacks must lay claim to, and visibly live, blackness. Furthermore, if passing as white is a specifically *American* phenomenon, as Davis suggests, then the logic of passing has been possible given a particular definition of race (that is, the notion of race constructed through the one-drop rule). If being black has meant "having one drop of black blood,"[9] then passing has meant stepping outside of that strict categorization. It has meant not allowing one's black blood to show.[10]

A white-imposed system of segregation, such as that instituted by Jim Crow, demonstrated an anxiety that whites would find themselves "tainted" by black blood. The Jim Crow system, combined with the one-drop rule, revealed the fear of whites that blacks would enter "their" place and challenge white identity. It also divulged an anxiety that whites would be revealed as black; that is, it disclosed a fear that whites would be found to contain some "invisible 'black blood' " (Davis 1993, 77). This fear is one of (bodily) "bleeding"—anxiety that an oppositional term would overextend its set framework. Hence, the logic behind racial segregation mimics the washing directions on the tag of a white bath towel: "Wash dark or bright colors separately as they may 'bleed' and discolor other articles." Anxiety over "discoloring," fear that one's own white color would be thrown into question through its mixing with Other (darker) colors, has necessitated separate spheres. The horror for whites is to be consumed by blackness. Of course, the irony behind this fear is that whites themselves have been the consumers (cf. hooks 1992).

A related consequence of the one-drop rule is, as Davis remarks, that "racially mixed" has not "been an accepted racial category in the United States for a child who has any black ancestry at all" (1993, 129); rather, "One is either white or black" (129). The issue of blood or bleeding again arises in this context in that laws against miscegenation have been laws against the mixing and blurring of the races. Davis indicates that "[t]he mixing of what are presumed to be superior stocks with 'inferior' and detested stocks allegedly leads to *blood poisoning* and other physical deterioration, to mental inferiority, and to immorality and cultural degeneracy" (1993, 25). "White" blood, like the white bath towel, is thought to be contaminated by "black" blood or dark colors. It could even be maintained that white fear of contamination of/by the blood is, in essence, indicative of a broader Western fear of the fluid. The shoring up of binary terms has meant that in-between categories have been excluded as viable positions of subjectivity. Racial mixing has, in turn, raised basic questions vis-à-vis traditional interpretations of identity. To be strictly neither one term nor the other is to be asked, "What *are* you?" This metaphysical question has precisely been premised upon a conception of race as exclusive and oppositional.

Laurie Shrage indicates that the category of *racially mixed*, while being granted limited literary reference, has only existed in tragic manifestations. However, Shrage suggests that "[i]f freed from these stigmas, the visibility of mixed-race, or multiply or ambiguously raced, persons might challenge a racial system that otherwise maintains the fictions of racial and ethnic purity" (1997, 184). As mappings of white cultures/white bodies and white cultures/black bodies do not render the same meanings, neither do sexual relations between white/white and white/black subjects. If desire has always been given the telos of the child, then the more precise goal of the sexual relation has been the "unblemished child." Conceived on a traditional procreative model, the object of sexual desire must be someone of a *different* sex but of the *same* race. This demand for both difference and sameness is premised upon the idea that sexual relations between members of different sexes affords offspring, while sexual relations between members of like races affords (racially) *pure* offspring.

In the case of antimiscegenation laws, however, the logic is even more complicated than white fear of boundary bleeding, since under these very laws whites have been allowed to cross lines that blacks have not. That is, "many of the same male protectors of white womanhood helped mold the Jim Crow practice of sexual exploitation of black females by white males, thus contributing to miscegenation while they were fighting to keep the races pure" (Davis 1993, 55). While black men have been denied access to white women, white men have afforded themselves access to black women, since "coercive sexual relations with black women symbolized white male dominance and black male powerlessness" (Davis 1993, 54). As hooks remarks, beginning in slavery, "black women's bodies were the discursive terrain, the playing fields where racism and sexuality converge" (57). The convergence of racism and sexuality can also be seen in the interpretation of black female bodies offered by nineteenth-century medical discourse, inasmuch as racist interpretations of black female bodies underscored construals of black women's sexuality. Within the United States, hooks reminds us, "white men were legally declared 'insane' because they wanted to marry black slave women with whom they were sexually and romantically involved" (hooks 1992, 58). However, hooks further observes:

> As historical narrative [the insanity of white men] was long ago supplanted by the creation of another story. That story, invented by white men, is about the overwhelming desperate longing black men have to sexually violate the bodies of white women. (58)

Hence, when viewed from the perspective of blacks, whites have easily been considered the "terrifying" and the "terrorizing" (cf. hooks 1992, 170). Perhaps not coincidentally, whites put into play a framework that narrates the opposite—the idea that blacks (in particular, black men) are dangerous and threatening Others. White ability to move where/while black bodies have been presumably contained is further illustrated by hooks's recounting from childhood, "The 'official' white men who came across the tracks to sell products, Bibles, and insurance . . . those white men who crossed our thresholds" (1992, 170). "The tracks"—whites residing on one side and blacks on the other—reinscribes an image of the races conceived as opposing binaries. "Crossing the threshold" gestures toward white exploitation of blacks. While whites could freely cross to the "segregated space of blackness," blacks were denied such mobility (hooks 1992, 170), for "the more intimate the contact between blacks and whites, the stronger the whites' feelings that segregation must be maintained" (Davis 1993, 60). Within an imposed structure of segregation—"the tracks" illustrating a literal split between black and white—to merely stand on those tracks and position oneself in-between realms of black and white would constitute a gesture of resistance.

Consequently, referring to Houston Baker's work, Diana Fuss relays that "the two figures that come to stand most certainly for difference are the railway roadhouse and the crossing sign" (1989, 87). For Baker, the railway roadhouse is "located at the center of the switchyard, [and] switches trains from track to track"; the crossing sign "functions as a signal for a certain Derridean notion of ceaseless movement and play" (Fuss 1989, 87). "The railway junction is marked by transience"—a "place betwixt and between" (87). Baker suggests that "the crossing sign is the antithesis of a place marker. It signifies, always, change, motion, transience, process" (1988, 202). Thus, to live in-between races is to bridge the oppositional by straddling the crossing.

THE WHITENESS OF SEXUAL DIFFERENCE

To return for a moment to Irigaray, it should be noted that in *I Love to You*, Irigaray states, "Sexual difference is an immediate natural given. The whole of humankind is composed of women and men and of nothing else. The problem of race is, in fact, a secondary problem" (1996, 47). Prior to Irigaray's explicit statement that race is secondary to sexual difference, her position on race can be inferred from her positing of sexual difference as ontological difference, as discussed earlier. Theorists such as Hammonds and Butler have highlighted problems with prioritizing sexual difference over other forms of difference, as well as of failing to articulate the role of race in constructions of sexuality and gender. Hammonds maintains:

> I could argue that while it has been acknowledged that "race" is not simply additive to, or derivative of sexual difference, few white feminists have attempted to move beyond simply stating this point to

describe the powerful effect that "race" has on the construction and representation of gender and sexuality. (1994, 127)

And Butler offers:

To claim that sexual difference is more fundamental than racial difference is effectively to assume that sexual difference is white sexual difference and that whiteness is not a form of racial difference. (1993, 181–82)

Irigaray's remark that "race is a secondary problem" (re)positions sexual difference in a site of privileged Otherness. That is, for Irigaray, the sexually different Other ("woman") is maintained as the Other par excellence.

Claims to "see" racial difference are often considered dangerous, since they easily issue forth visions of a conceived (white) superiority over a racially different Other. Thus, as noted above, white liberals often remark, "I don't see skin color." However, as hooks and others have argued, the (white) liberal view—that racism would cease to exist "if we all just forget about race" and view one another as the same—neglects the fact that we are not all the same. In so doing, the liberal view arguably maintains structures of white supremacy by ignoring systems of privilege and power that continually (re)center and (re)value whiteness. Moreover, the failure of whites to consider racial difference—and the very statement *not* to see skin color—belies the fact that skin color must indeed be "seen" in order to then deny that it has been noticed. Hence, professing not to see more likely seems to mark a refusal of awareness.

In this respect, and insofar as Irigaray prioritizes difference over sameness, she would not likely advocate a neglect of race. In other words, Irigaray is not easily read as a white liberal. Nevertheless, inasmuch as Irigaray explicitly maintains a secondary status for race, she problematically relegates race to a subordinate position vis-à-vis sexual difference. Irigaray does not consider the Otherness of racial difference to be as substantial, complex, or real as that of sexual difference. This not only positions racial difference as inferior to sexual difference, it also posits sexual difference as unmarked by race.

It can certainly be asked whether Irigaray's position on race is an outcome of her own white positioning. After all, to take lived bodies seriously means that even the views of lived body theorists are informed through their own lived bodies and experiences. However, to also keep with a notion of contingency means that while it is not necessarily true that one is locked into one's own subject position (unable to understand and articulate positions outside of it), neither is one's positioning arbitrary (unrelated to the views and understandings one precisely adopts). In a similar way, it is not necessary, but it is surely not accidental, that people of color are more likely than whites to refer to race as a central organizing category. Given that race connects to lived experiences, people of color are more likely to consider the dismissal or demotion of race as naïve and/or dangerous.

Gordon (1997) suggests that while white women stand in proximity to blackness by being similarly conceived as "absence, darkness, and lack," white women simultaneously risk betraying this contiguity in virtue of their whiteness. Despite the potential for coalition building between black men and white women, there is no relation of symmetry between *black* men and white *women*. Gordon's account indicates the impossibility of ever separating sex from race, and it can be further illustrated by noting that while the commonality between black men and white women is rooted in black men's blackness (that is, their race) and white women's femaleness (that is, their sex), the contrariety between them is anchored in black men's maleness (that is, their sex) and white women's whiteness (that is, their race). Consequently, race and sex relate in ways that render both similarity and difference, and the nature of the relation between racially different men and women is not easily simplified. Instead, racial differences suggest a complexity of relation that must be examined in considering sexual difference. This interweaving of sexual and racial difference is clearly neglected in the work of Irigaray and other theorists of sexual difference.

Thus, Irigaray's remark that "race is a secondary problem" indeed supports Butler's charge that sexual difference theory may, in fact, employ the category of sexual difference as neutral—thereby implicitly relying upon a white conception of sexual difference. Relatedly, Irigaray also appears, as Patricia Huntington claims, to "perpetuate 'white authorial presence'" (1997, 189). Seeing that one of Irigaray's expressed concerns is to reveal sites in which presumed neutral concepts are actually masculine in construction (for example, "the subject," desire, and language), the act of construing sexual difference as an unmarked category when it is precisely marked as white is especially damaging for Irigarayan theory. While Irigaray recovers a "feminine presence" from the Western tradition (that is, a *white* feminine presence), she simultaneously conspires in a "racial absence."

Hammonds has remarked that "[b]lack feminist theorists have almost universally described women's sexuality, when viewed from the vantage of the dominant discourse, as an absence" (1994, 131). Western thought, instituting itself at the level of ontology, is perpetuated by systems based on analogous logic at the level of social and political theory. Stated another way, Western thought itself—and not simply discriminatory practices—is inherently racist. Or, we could say that the specific structure of thought in the West implies racism. Consequently, absence within discourse does not merely occur on a continuum and is not simply additive (for example, "woman" . . . "black" . . . "black woman" . . .), since each category differently intersects with sexuality and gender to constitute the subject. While each pairing (for example, heterosexual/homosexual, white/black, men/women, white women/black women) represents a set of dichotomous terms, these pairs cannot be adequately considered in isolation from the others. According to Hammonds, black women face "a situation in which black women's sexuality is ideologically located in a nexus between 'race' and gender, where the black female subject is not seen and has no voice" (1994, 133).

In comparing black women's sexualities to the scientific black hole, Hammonds suggests that the existence of black women's sexualities is like the black hole in that they are evidenced "by [their] effects on the region of space where [they] are located" (1994, 138). Hammonds notes that "the existence of the black hole is inferred from the fact that the visible star is in orbit and its shape is distorted in some way" by something not seen (139). She asks how black women's sexualities, which linger in a void, affect what is visible (white women's sexualities), and conversely, how "the structure of what is visible, namely white women's sexualities, shape those not-absent-though-not-present black women's sexualities" (130–31).

While Hammonds emphasizes that she "was disturbed by the fact that the use of the image of a black hole could also evoke a negative image of black women's sexualities reduced to their lowest possible denominator, i.e. just a 'hole' " (1994, 142 n 8), the ability of the black hole image to evoke such a view of black women's sexualities is indicative of the hole or void conceived in terms of mere empty space. However, if "the void" is not construed as simply passive or empty, then the rendering of black women's sexualities as a void actually posits their ability to shape what is encountered. It suggests an activity to black women's sexualities, despite the invisibility and silence under which they are normally constituted. Black women's sexualities—their *bodies*—reside in-between presence and absence, race and gender. Hammonds indicates, "Black feminist theorists are themselves engaged in a process of fighting to reclaim the body" (1994, 134). *These* bodies—black women's bodies—appear problematically missing from sexual difference accounts. As a consequence, it can be questioned (perhaps rhetorically), upon whose experience sexual difference theory is premised and whose bodies serve as the models for these theoretical constructs.

CHAPTER FOUR

TRANSGENDER BODIES

▬▬▬▬▬▬▬▬▬▬▬▬▬▬▬▬▬▬▬▬

"He-she" and "she-male" describe the person's gender expression with the first pronoun and the birth sex with the second. The hyphenation signals a crisis of language and an apparent social contradiction, since sex and gender expression are "supposed" to match.

—Feinberg 1996

It wasn't as simple as my doctors made it sound. In the hospital, I turned control of my face over to my roommate Donna. She wanted to help. She tried to pinpoint exactly why my fifteen-year-old girl-face looked boyish. This turned out to be a bigger question than we could answer.

—Scholinski 1997

BODY THEORY AND DISEMBODIMENT

In addition to critiques concerning the whiteness of sexual difference theory, a disturbing claim has been made about much bodily theorizing in general— that body theory is often strangely *dis*embodied. Kathy Davis remarks on this strangeness, for example, when she writes, "theorizing about the body has all too often been a cerebral, esoteric, and ultimately, disembodied activity. The danger is that theories on the body distance us from individuals' everyday embodied experiences" (1997, 14). Rather than problematically theorizing from one's limited embodied experience, as discussed in relation to Irigaray in the previous chapter, the danger of disembodiment implies a replication of the Cartesian mind-body split whereby "the body" is ironically investigated from a position of detachment. As Susan Wendell points out:

"The body" is often discussed as a cultural construction, and the body or body parts are taken to be symbolic forms in a culture. In

59

this latter development, experience of the body is at best left out of discussion, and at worst precluded by the theory; here feminist theory itself is alienated from the body. (1996, 324)

Much like the alienation from bodies that has occurred through feminism's somatophobia, the detachment here involves the fact that when bodies have been investigated (as new theoretical "objects"), the tendency has been to theorize them in a starkly typical manner.

The so-called detachment of body theories from the bodies they theorize is also expressed by Carol Bigwood, who states, "[T]he poststructuralist body is so fluid it can take on almost limitless embodiments. It has no real terrestrial *weight*" (1991, 50). Bigwood's concern is with a neglect of bodily materiality, and with a lack of "anchoring" for bodies, within new understandings of "the subject" enabled by poststructuralism. A comparable point is made by Bibi Bakare-Yusuf who asks:

> What of the body that is always under the seduction of death, white racist violence, diseases, perverse heterosexism, pervasive addictions and unemployment? I am talking about the body that is marked by racial, sexual and class configurations. It is this body, this fleshy materiality that seems to disappear from much of the current proliferation of discourses on the body. (1999, 313)

Given such points of contention, it can be said that if body theory is often disembodied, then despite the potential for (and claims in favor of) conceptual transgression, bodily theorizing would not noticeably depart from traditional theoretical frameworks.

Oftentimes, remarks on theoretical detachment occur within general cautions regarding postmodern theory. While supporting the move away from strictly traditional understandings of the subject, the concern remains that postmodernism might extend the analysis too far. Consider, for instance, the following disclaimer introducing María Lugones's essay, "Purity, Impurity, and Separation":

> Note to the reader: This writing is done from within a hybrid imagination, within a recently articulate tradition of latina writers who emphasize mestizaje and multiplicity as tied to resistant and liberatory possibilities. All resemblance between this tradition and postmodern literature and philosophy is coincidental. (1996, 275)

Lugones aims to point out that reconceiving positionalities as liberatory and resistant potentials demands an attachment—to place, to location, to geography, to home—in ways contrary to a thoroughgoing postmodern antiessentialism and disengagement of the subject. Regarding the connection between bodies and postmodernism, Jacquelyn Zita makes a similar point, when she states, "Postmodernism is right in bringing into focus the contingency of sex identity imposed on and incorporated into the body's soma but wrong in supposing these to be lightweight and detachable" (1998, 107). Here, Zita comments on ways in which bodies and the category *sex*, while being open to experiential possibilities, must nonetheless be grounded. That is, while bodies are capable of assuming various sex/gender configurations, bodies are also socially and historically constrained. As a serious example of this point, we can note that anti-queer/anti-trans violence serves to indicate and to remind us of the weightiness and historical gravity of bodies, since no one is able to beat or to murder a detached and disembodied body. Queer/trans bodies do not exist devoid of context or sociohistorical import, and it is precisely from within certain anti-queer/anti-trans contexts that anti-queer/anti-trans violence assumes its possibility and meaning.

In this respect, and as one final example of distress over disembodied theory, Leslie Feinberg maintains in *Transgender Warriors*:

> Today, a great deal of "gender theory" is abstracted from human experience. But if theory is not the crystallized resin of experience, it ceases to be a guide to action. I offer history, politics, and theory that are rooted in the experience of real people who fought flesh-and-blood battles for freedom. (1996, xiii)

In this passage, Feinberg criticizes high queer theory for its disconnection from ordinary queer lives. Feinberg's concern directly connects to matters of praxis and politics which become ineffectual, for Feinberg, if untied from the lives of those involved.[1] Feinberg suggests that while high queer theory may locate "queerness" in texts, and postmodernism may reveal the queer body's "invention," both queer theory and postmodernism neglect (queer) bodies in their real, concrete, living—and sometimes dying—manifestations.

QUESTIONING SEXUAL DIFFERENCE

As body theories, I propose, sexual difference theories have the virtue of not being postmodern theories. Or, we could say, perhaps more accurately, that sexual difference theories avoid what Zita views as "wrong" with postmodernism. While sexual difference analyses are precisely theories of the body, given the centrality of a notion of *lived* bodies within these accounts, bodies as lived are—by definition—not detached bodies. Positioned in-between the biological (body) and the social (culture), lived bodies transcend the body's mere biology. At the same time, lived bodies do not float off into a disembodied space (that is, away from ordinary, corporeal, and lived experiences). Instead, as has been noted in previous chapters, lived bodies are both situated and not easily fixed, positioned and not easily located, identified and not easily categorized. Within sexual difference frameworks, then, bodies are articulated as phenomena neither static nor free-floating. Consequently, sexual difference theories both loosen the limitations on bodies (and the relation between sex and gender) while they posit the conditions for these very constraints in the first place.

However, while in-between positions—as exemplified by lived bodies—can offer liberating and resistant potential, to exist in-between extremes is often difficult for individuals materially situated there. As Ann duCille remarks in a different context, "One of the dangers of standing at an intersection is the likelihood of being run over by oncoming traffic" (1996, 72). In the present case, this means that living one's body within an often unrecognized social and theoretical space means being relegated to the "outside" of prescribed and binary boundaries of demarcation. To identify—or to be perceived—as transgendered, for instance, means to embody a "violation" of static conceptions of identity.[2] Importantly, theories of sexual difference highlight the possibility that if bodies—*all* bodies—always exceed "their own boundaries," as Butler specifically states, and if bodies are never static and polarized (despite mainstream Western ideas to the contrary), then transgendered subjects make this persistent excess clear. Trans-bodies transgress and threaten compartmentalized dichotomous/dualistic borders. They reveal that many presumed polarities are never quite polar and that identity itself is always already a matter of bleeding and extension.

Gender Transgression and Generated Puzzles

To return for a moment to the opening concerns about theoretical detachment, it still appears possible to ask the following question of sexual difference theories: If sexual difference theories presumably focus on lived bodies, and trans-bodies are lived bodies that nicely exemplify sexual difference theories, but sexual difference theories do not explicitly address trans-experiences, then do sexual difference theories err or contradict themselves in virtue of this (and other) neglect(s)? The puzzle I see is as follows: On the one hand, it seems that the very existence of trans-people forces a rethinking of concepts such as the meaning and function of gender, the normative nature of sex/gender mappings, and the various complexities of sexual/social identities. On the other hand, it seems that sexual difference theories offer analyses and understandings of an engrained refusal to tolerate non-normative subject/body positions. Thus, it can be asked whether *theories about* bodies have any force without bodies and lives to which they might attach. And it can be questioned whether there is a proper role for theory in furthering the sort of "dichotomy challenge" that is evidenced by the way many people live their bodies on a daily basis.

Gatens clearly makes the proposal of at least two kinds of bodies when she states, "There are at least two bodies; the male body and the female body" (1991, 145). Sexual difference theories *are* sexual difference theories, at least in part, by way of this recognition. Gatens's observation is a claim against what she calls the presumed neutrality of the body (again, the idea that bodies are mere blank slates). While this point has been very significant for feminist theory, I nonetheless wish to raise a few questions in relation to theories of sexual difference. First, I would like to ask how sexual difference theories, following the insight of two sexually different bodies, might take up a case in which the very question of what constitutes a male or female body itself has been troubled. That is, how would sexual difference theories engage with Loren Cameron, a trans-man whose self-portraits depict a sexed body itself in a state of perpetual transition? Cameron's self-portraits, in *Body Alchemy* (1996), do not neatly fit within traditional categories of *male* and *female*. Aspects of Cameron's body emerge as male, while others emanate as female, suggesting that both sexes can coexist within one bodily inscription.

Moreover, there is a refusal in the case of Cameron, to completely transition—in terms of his body—to the so-called opposite sex. This state of affairs renders implausible any easy notion of two mutually exclusive categories (male and female), since Cameron's portraits demonstrate that there is no male *or* female body; rather, male and female are themselves in states of flux and fluidity. In addition, the presence of physical scars indicates a reminder or remainder of gender transition. As the navel serves as a memento of birth (of attachment to and detachment from the mother), the surgical scars of sex reassignment connect bodily past and present.

Secondly, as discussed in chapter 3, Butler raises the question of whether an emphasis on the irreducibility of sexual difference acts to prioritize sexual difference over other forms of difference, including racial difference—thereby relying, implicitly, on a white notion of sexual difference. I see this point as particularly valid when we consider that certain traditional dichotomies—such as "male" and "female," or stereotypes of "male activity" and "female passivity"—do not consider other classic stereotypes of specific nonwhite racialized identities; for example, the emasculated ("passive") Asian/Asian American man, or the super-strong ("active") African American woman. Consequently, male activity and female passivity are most likely raced concepts—raced, primarily it seems, as white. In fact, part of the grotesque nature of the U.S. "mammy" stereotype, for instance, involved the fact that through this image, black women were aligned more with (white) masculinity than with (white) femininity. Black women were regarded as "unnatural" on this basis (that is, on the basis of a heightened activity). Or rather, the stereotype of the "mammy" itself offered a means by which to reinforce an already-determined and professed inferiority of black women.

Thirdly, I wonder how—or rather, *do*—sexual difference theories treat intersections between the lived categories of sex/gender, race, sexuality, class, ability, nationality, etc. I wonder what sexual difference theories would say about the scenario opening David Eng and Alice Hom's *Q&A: Queer in*

Asian America (1998)? In the real-life example, a white woman "mistakes" a butch-looking Asian American lesbian for an Asian/Asian American man in a public women's restroom. Given mainstream racial(ized) and sexual(ized) stereotypes about Asian women and men, the Asian American lesbian is not seen as a lesbian; rather, she is seen as an emasculated Asian American man—who, the white woman "racistly" presumes, must be in the women's restroom because he cannot read English.[3] Here, invisibility cannot be ascribed to sexual difference in any easy way. While the scenario involves theoretically interesting notions concerning ambiguity, for instance, the white woman's resolution of the situation fails to register that ambiguity. It is not a case, in Eng and Hom's example, of "having to decide" a perceived ambiguity one way or the other; instead, it is a matter of failing to perceive what is more ambiguous than one decides.

Concerning the intersection between trans-experience and race, it could be noted that a black woman who transitions to the identity of a black man is not socially positioned in the same way as a white woman who transitions to the position of a white man. In the case of a black female-to-male (FTM) transsexual, it could be argued that while he gains male privilege, he also inherits negative stereotypes associated with black men. Thus, the black FTM's daily experiences alter drastically, not simply in relation to an unmarked construction of gender, but precisely with respect to the way in which gender is likewise "raced." In the case of a white female-to-male transsexual, it could be argued that his position is actually advanced; that is, he continues to benefit from white privilege, while he gains the added benefit of male privilege. I will return to this issue in chapter 6, since from a transsexual perspective, there are some added complications that must be considered with these examples.

With regard to the three main questions asked above, however, it is quite possible that all three of these questions may be answered in a similar manner. First, it seems that by highlighting the lived body and its persistent bleeding, sexual difference theories are quite equipped to address the sexed ambiguity (both male and female) exemplified by Cameron and others. Nonetheless, given an emphasis on two sexually different subjects, we may still ask whether sexual difference theories go far enough. That is to say, does the lived body of Cameron push beyond much theorizing on bodily inbetweenness? If so, then shouldn't such body practices precisely inform body theories? Secondly, inasmuch as sexual difference theories assume the primacy of sex and explicitly exclude discussion of race, they may still be criticized for failing to adequately address racial difference. While sexual difference theories open areas of theoretical possibility and critique how particular subject positions have been rendered invisible, we may still ask whether these concerns are sufficiently complicated—complicated by race, class, and sexuality, for example.

Considering Possibilities

In arguing against assumptions of bodies as neutral, Gatens argues against what she calls "the postulated *arbitrary* connection between femininity and the female body; masculinity and the male body" (1991, 140). Again, Gatens suggests that the relation between categories must be examined—remarking that "[g]ender is not the issue, sexual difference is" (145). This claim indicates, contra gender feminists, that patriarchy is not a system that valorizes the masculine gender over the feminine gender; rather, patriarchal structures value the masculine *male*. The sexed body residing behind the gender expression, in other words, is of vast importance. The fact that different meanings are attributed to various sex-gender mappings becomes clear when we consider our everyday awareness that the significance of a female body's masculinity differs from a female body's femininity, and a male body's masculinity differs from a male body's femininity. We could say that anti-queer/anti-trans violence, such as the murders of Brandon Teena,[4] Eddie (Gwen) Araujo, and many unpublicized others, is a precise consequence of these different meanings and the demand that "normal" mappings be maintained. Likewise, the diagnosis "Gender Identity Disorder"[5] can exist for this same reason, permitting the institutionalization of people like Daphne Scholinski who do not adhere to "normal" sex-gender combinations. Not accidentally, then, both the murderer and the psychiatric institution mark two sites of trans-"treatment."

Moreover, if bleeding and extension are aspects of *all* identities, and if identities are *never* clearly demarcated, then trans-subjects reveal a great deal to non-trans people. Scholinski demonstrates much, for example, that the (gender congruent) mental health professionals fail to adequately consider. Relaying her interactions with a patient named Bob, who identifies himself as Jesus, Scholinski remarks:

> The more I talked to Jesus, the more I liked him, and the less crazy he seemed. I could imagine him in the outside world, preaching. He'd probably help some people. This posed an interesting dilemma: If I thought he was sane, what did that make me? Mental hospitals are rife with this kind of debate. . . . The staff discouraged this sort of questioning. They liked the line between sane and insane to be perfectly clear. (1997, 19)

Scholinski's observation connects back, I think, with what Zita finds "right" with postmodernism, for Zita's comments on the "rightness" and "wrongness" of postmodern thinking are contained in her essay, "Male Lesbians and the Postmodernist Body." The question of the male lesbian—like the case of "Jesus"—offers no easy answers, since simply responding "yes" or "no" to suggestions of delusion does not adequately address the ways in which identities are fluid. As Zita states:

> The paradox of the "male lesbian" reveals some insights into how sex identity attributions are customarily established for all of us in our culture. The range of lived interpretations for the body is less determined by anatomy and more determined by the interpretations and prescriptions given to that anatomy. (1998, 105)

Likewise, I suggest, postmodernism makes the mental-patient-as-Jesus a serious consideration. However, to also incorporate constraints—such as those offered by sexual difference theories—means that Bob is most likely *both* Jesus *and* not-Jesus. A "both . . . and . . ." identity is importantly tied to both the fluidity and the historical gravity of the body subject.

An additional connection can be made, here, to Judith Halberstam's (1998) work on female masculinity in that Halberstam conveys:

> A great example of denaturalized identification was featured as a comic device in the 1995 movie *Babe*. Babe depicts the triumph of function over form when the pig, Babe, proves to be a better sheepdog than a sheepdog. The success of Babe's dog performance depends on assumption of the role "dog" with a difference. Whereas the master sheepdog presumes his superiority over the sheep, Babe refuses to construct a new hierarchy or to preserve natural hierarchies; instead, he proves his willingness and ability to herd and show proper respect for the sheep and above all takes pleasure in his dogness. (255)

Babe is a " 'sheepdog' with a difference." Babe reconfigures the sheepdog identity by *both* enacting *and* displacing it. The question of whether Babe could be disqualified from sheep-herding competition, on grounds that he is not a "real" sheepdog, is an important question. Indeed, self-identified male lesbians have been at times excluded from "the lesbian community proper" on grounds that they are not "real" lesbians. However, could a male lesbian prove to be a better lesbian than a (female bodied) lesbian?; and should a male lesbian be excluded from lesbian communities a priori? If the movie *Babe* is radical, its departure from the ordinary resides in its allowing Babe, a pig, not only to adopt a sheepdog identity but to be rewarded for this transspecies assumption. Babe emerges a hero. Such trans-associated heroism stands in opposition to the verdict that the mental-patient-as-Jesus is delusional, or the command that Scholinski apply make-up and curl her hair to earn institutional points as "treatment" for her "disorder." Scholinski asks, with a dry sense of humor, that we look at her and determine whether the "treatment plan" was "effective."[6] If Scholinski *still* embodies boyishness—perhaps due to her very comfort and pleasure in such—then is this boyishness, too, " 'boyishness' with a difference"; and what *is* the difference?

A COYOTE IN SHEEP'S CLOTHING

Finally, it is important to note that while Scholinski considers herself to be gay, the identity *lesbian* is one with which Scholinski has struggled. Since Scholinski does not readily identify with the category *woman*, she also feels disconnected from the identity *lesbian*. But then, what about the male lesbian? Is the male lesbian "lesbian," at least in part, in virtue of relating to the category *woman*? Would "real" lesbians consider such a connection necessary for inclusion in the category *lesbian*? And could we imagine a case in which a person identifies as lesbian while precisely feeling disconnected from the category *woman*? Is such a person "delusional"? Could I, a seeming-woman, identify as a gay man? Is it clear and obvious that I cannot so identify because I am, after all, *not* a man? Must I be a man (or, have a male body) to identify as a gay man? And, what *is* a man?

As I continue to reflect on the Babe-as-sheepdog example, I am led to wonder what the movie's outcome would have been if the *cat*, instead of the pig, had assumed the sheepdog function. After all, cats, and not pigs, have been conceived as oppositional to dogs; and, isn't the male lesbian's exclusion from lesbian communities partially due to the presumed oppositional nature of male/female, men/women, male/lesbian? We could ask whether the cat's, rather than the pig's, good sheep-herding performance would have been equally valued and rewarded by the competition judges. Or, we could even ask whether the cat *could be* a (good) sheep herder. That is, would the fact of the cat's catness—or the historical gravity of the cat, or of the cat's body— trump any possibility for inclusion within the category *sheepdog*? Certainly, dogs have been set in opposition to cats in ways that our popular views do not mandate for pigs. Conversely, though, we could ask whether the cat could ever be a *better* sheepdog than a sheepdog. And, central to the project at hand, are these questions about fictional animals in a movie "strangely disembodied"? Are they merely "cerebral" and "esoteric"? Do they act to insult real-life human experiences?

Thinking that the answer to these last questions is likely both "yes" and "no," I will risk closing with the example of Wiley Coyote—who, in the *Roadrunner* cartoons, zips himself into the skin of a sheep in order to blend in with the flock. Since coyotes are constructed as predatory—and in this sense as oppositional—in relation to sheep (as men are to women), the context for this particular sheep (rather than sheepdog) assumption is of vast significance. Indeed, considerations of context often make a huge difference in asking and answering questions about community inclusion and exclusion. Context can be said to offer constraints on our identity notions; and the historical gravity of bodies is central to how context is construed. After all, is it not from within a context of a history of "lesbian separatism" and/or of "woman-only spaces" that the so-called male lesbian is rendered particularly suspicious? Is not the weightiness of the male lesbian's body highlighted by these very circumstances? The male lesbian is perceived, it could be said, as a coyote in sheep's clothing. Is this a real sheep, or a potentially dangerous imposter? Moreover, does a formula to the effect of "lesbian = woman + sleeps with women" contribute to the uproar and community boundary re-inforcement that occurs when a self-identified (female) lesbian sleeps with a man?[7] Is the woman who sleeps with a man *really* a lesbian? Is she a " 'lesbian' with a difference"? What factors, in this scenario, serve to constitute a reply? And, as others have asked of similar phenomena, what is the force of the "really"—or of the *real*—in the first place?[8]

CHAPTER FIVE

COMPETING NARRATIVES
IN LGBTQ STUDIES

CHANGING SEXUALITIES, CHANGING PEDAGOGIES: MUST IDENTITY PEDAGOGIES SELF-DESTRUCT?

The question above plays on Gamson's (1998) question, "Must identity movements self destruct?" in his article on the emergence of queer politics and their significance to a lesbian/gay/bisexual/transgender (LGBT) identity politics.[1] Another way that Gamson phrases his question is as follows: "If identities are indeed much more unstable, fluid and constructed than movements have tended to assume—if one takes the queer challenge seriously, that is—what happens to identity-based social movements such as gay and lesbian rights?" (1998, 590). Gamson's question could be rephrased again to ask the following question about pedagogy: "If identities are indeed much more unstable, fluid and constructed than pedagogies have tended to assume—if one takes the queer challenge seriously, that is—what happens to identity-based (standpoint) pedagogies such as feminist or lesbian and gay pedagogies?"

Gamson answers his own question by asserting that it is not important to determine which logic (a deconstructive or quasi-ethnic one) is more appropriate for social movement organizing or for LGBTQ political goals. Rather, he argues that both "logics" make sense. As he explains, collective identity categories are "both necessary and damaging" in today's American political environment. Consequently, it makes sense to engage strategies of both identity and anti-identity in a contemporary politics of sexualities.[2] In the present chapter, I build upon the idea of an important interplay between identity and anti-identity in social movements by bringing the discussion into the classroom—specifically, the lesbian and gay studies classroom within

69

institutions of higher education in the United States.[3] At heart, I argue that
the changing nature of understandings about the social organization of human
sexualities necessitates not an end to identity pedagogies, but an instantiation
of new performances of them.

Identity Pedagogies

> Teaching an introduction to lesbian and gay studies (course) may seem like
> a natural for someone who calls herself a lesbian and a feminist, and indeed,
> when I was offered the chance to teach such a course, I leapt at the oppor-
> tunity. However, teaching in that new and growing field presents problems
> for those who claim lesbian and/or feminist identities.

> —Plymire 2000

The problem that Plymire identifies involves the way that feminisms are
maligned by queer texts because of an investment, in some sense, in stable
identities. Her observation points to the lesbian and gay studies classroom as
a political arena in which the end of identity politics and the queering of
identity have problematized the "simple" task of teaching lesbian and gay
studies. I engage this puzzle by maintaining that it is important to employ *both*
identity *and* anti-identity "logics" within this particular classroom site. I begin
by discussing how pedagogical strategies for teaching a class such as lesbian and
gay studies have been pedagogies of identity—philosophies of teaching derived
from identity politics and rooted in standpoint epistemology.

Feminist Standpoint Pedagogies

> Feminist theory and pedagogy are distinct from other forms of theory/peda-
> gogy in their focus on women and women's diversity of experience, how
> these experiences contextualize and inform knowledge, and how the class-
> room can be constructed to involve students as teacher-learner—inviting
> students to become active participants in their own educations.

> —Sandler, Silverberg, and Hall in Cohee et al. 1998

Characterizing feminist pedagogies is a complex task since they are as varied
as the types of feminisms themselves.[4] In addition, they tend to be rather
unstable in that teachers use various pedagogical strategies depending upon
the context and classroom, stage in one's career, and one's social location or
"identity." Yet, discussions of feminist pedagogies often assume the following
core components: consciousness raising or building a critical consciousness as
part of teaching; examining the place of the personal in learning; redefining
authority—especially between teacher and students—in the classroom; creating a transformative knowledge for concrete social change; empowering
and liberating students (with an emphasis on the subordination of women,

people "of color," the working class/poor, and LGBT individuals); and examining global systems of domination (in the form of white supremacy, capitalism, imperialism, colonialism, sexism, and homophobia/heterosexism) (Cohee et al. 1998). Conceptions of feminist pedagogies often have been derived from the works of Paulo Freire (cf. hooks 1994; Wright 1998), who identified the "banking style" of teaching as one that reproduces dynamics of domination and subordination in the classroom. Freire has illustrated how the very philosophies of teaching about domination and subordination have been complicit in the reproduction of oppression (McLaren 1997). In sum, feminist theories assume that the precise ways in which we construct knowledge and teach it are based on systems of domination. Feminist pedagogies seek to destabilize such paradigms in the classroom and in the teaching of feminist theoretical ideas.

In many ways, the types of feminist pedagogies described above may be classified as modern in their notions of liberation, identity, and consciousness (McLaren 1997, 151). In fact, these very characteristics of feminist pedagogies suggest a feminist standpoint epistemology; that is, the assumption that women with a critical feminist consciousness are better able to see systems of domination and understand dynamics of sexism than those without such a stance. The underlying belief, here, is that one's everyday life has epistemological consequences and implications—the disadvantaged having the potential to be more knowledgeable, in a way, than the dominant group (Harding 1987). As Cohee et al. remark, "Feminist pedagogy emphasizes the development of epistemological frameworks that stress both the subjective and communal reality of knowing" (1998, 3). Consequently, the very notion of a feminist pedagogy assumes a way of knowing and learning rooted in lived experience and identity.

If we consider that many of our conceptions of feminist pedagogies still rely on and reproduce modernist ideas, then we interestingly face postmodern and queer critiques (as suggested by Plymire 2000). Indeed, feminist standpoint pedagogies can be critiqued for employing an essentialism (a collective identity and consciousness) concomitant with a modernist view of oppression. Within such a framewok, the fluidity of identity categories and the exclusive dangers of identity politics go unrecognized (Mann and Kelley 1997). Thus, we could ask whether a feminist standpoint pedagogy should be employed in the teaching of lesbian and gay studies. If we use such a pedagogy, what are we implicitly teaching? Are we not, in some sense, teaching identity politics and producing the very categories of identity that have been problematized by postmodern and queer theory?

Lesbian and Gay Pedagogy

There is an important function for those educators who are willing and able to self-identify as lesbian or gay. Societal hatred, fear and misunderstanding are focused on the stereotyped images of gay and lesbian. One way of diffusing the potency of those labels is by redefining them, reframing them, so that they lose their negative power.

—Wright 1998

Similar to the diversity of feminist pedagogies, "lesbian and gay pedagogy" is not a unified project. However, as an endeavor, it certainly seems to hold identity logic as central. In general, lesbian and gay pedagogy seeks to explain how best to teach students an understanding of homophobia and heterosexism. Notably, most discussions of lesbian and gay pedagogy focus on questions of "coming out" (or claiming a lesbian or gay identity) within the classroom. Whether examining the utility of instructors coming out to their classes (Wright 1998), having students write a coming out letter, using the "pink triangle exercise" (Chesler 1991), inviting LGBT guest speakers to come out on a "speaker's bureau" (Berg et al. 1998), or assigning anthologies of coming out stories as class texts (Wright 1998), discussions of lesbian and gay pedagogy have assumed the pivotal importance of LGBT identity work in the classroom. Like feminist standpoint pedagogy, lesbian and gay pedagogy assumes a standpoint—by gay people for gay people—and maintains liberatory goals (that is, LGBT liberation). And so, teaching about LGBT experience has been rooted in a pedagogy of identity, where an LGBT standpoint is figured as central.[5]

Indeed, lesbian and gay pedagogy is difficult to separate from feminist standpoint pedagogies insofar as they share a common assumption about standpoint epistemology and liberatory perspectives of identity politics. In fact, many discussions of feminist pedagogy include essays on coming out and the politics thereof (cf. Cohee et al. 1998). It is fairly clear, then, that our women's studies and lesbian and gay studies classrooms have been constructed as sites of identity. As such, the question of how to teach a lesbian and gay studies course attendant to new understandings of sexualities and politics resonates. Plymire's (2000) dilemma of how to teach a lesbian and gay studies class, while identifying as a lesbian and a feminist and attending to queer theory's very complication of these identities, can be viewed as highlighting this very question. Plymire's remarks highly symbolize the emergence of new understandings of sexualities and the need to reevaluate the use of identity pedagogies. While there is a draw to the logic behind feminist and lesbian and gay identity pedagogies, there is also an increasing awareness that such pedagogies must be further complicated.

Beyond Identity Pedagogies: Queer Pedagogies

Queering (pedagogy) means that students should see that sexual identity categories aren't fixed. This makes many students, queer or not, uncomfortable. Teaching about sexuality means talking about sexuality. This makes many teachers uncomfortable. Add the desire and ethical necessity to teach against homophobia . . . the need to represent multiple differences . . . and the difficulty of not privileging experiential knowledge . . . and just choosing a class exercise can be formidable.

—Wallace 1994

Framing an examination of queer pedagogy, Seidman (1994, 169) poses two questions helpful to an examination of teaching beyond identity. First, he asks, "Does queerness suggest a pedagogy?," and second, he offers, "What difference does homosexual desire or a gay/lesbian identity make in teaching?" Answering the first of these questions, Seidman confounds the notion that queerness implies a particular "identity" out of which a "standpoint" emerges, since this idea would be at odds with the deconstructive move of queer theory and politics. Seidman complicates the idea of coming out in the classroom as a liberatory strategy. However, responding to his second question, Seidman makes a heartfelt argument for the necessity of "queering" academic work through the inclusion of more LGBT-identified scholars and courses on LGBT experience—arguing that in an institutional and social climate of invisibility and silence, there is still merit in "exposing the reality of intolerance beneath the veil of liberal academic culture of tolerance" (1994, 173). Through these questions and answers, Seidman demonstrates the pull of identity politics and standpoint epistemologies in lesbian and gay studies *and* the significance of queer theory's complications of them. Ultimately, he concludes that there is a danger in resorting to a queer standpoint pedagogy without also illustrating the "minoritizing" logic of identity politics and the epistemological consequences of standpoint ideas.

Seidman's (1994) consideration of a queer pedagogy highlights the tension we often feel in the lesbian and gay studies classroom between the competing necessities of engaging identity politics by creating a space that engages coming out and breaking the silence and that constructs gay and lesbian knowledges, on the one hand, and recognizing the danger of essentializing gender and sexuality, replicating rigid identity categories and politics, and failing to theorize heteronormativity, on the other hand. As Wallace articulates this paradox: "How do instructors teach against heterosexism and about gay and lesbian lives without reinforcing essentialist ideas about sexuality?" (1994, 181). The challenge for queer pedagogies, first and foremost, is how to attend to the "both necessary and damaging" task of shoring up the categories while also smashing them (Gamson 1998). Simply stated, the identity categories of homo/lesbian/gay are each imbued with multiple meanings, politics, and theories—all of which figure in the articulation of a "queer" pedagogy (Seidman 1994, 173).

Despite the complications of identifying queer universals (Jagose 1997), there are some central pedagogical points highlighted by queer activists, scholars, and theorists. For example, Seidman remarks that queer pedagogies must "refuse a preoccupation with the making of homo/lesbian/gay identities and communities in favor of strategies that trace the operation of homosexuality in dominant codes and conventions of straight society" (1994, 176). He recommends putting homosexuality at center, "as present wherever heterosexuality operates" (176). Wallace adds that a queer pedagogy would "explicitly acknowledge the connection between knowledge and power," "focus on how sexuality and sexual regimes are reproduced," and "acknowledge the instability of all sexual identity categories" (1994, 179–80). Most writing about queer pedagogy agrees that teaching from both a minoritizing model of identity and a queer critique of those very identity categories is the best means by which to enact a queer pedagogy today (cf. Seidman 1994; Wallace 1994; Zimmerman 1996).

In sum, queer pedagogy has been framed as needing to employ classroom strategies of both identity and anti-identity in order to address both the draw of identity politics and standpoint epistemologies in lesbian and gay studies, *and* the complications of these "identities" and "standpoints" by queer theory. This logic recognizes that the sociohistorical moment and institutional structure in the United States calls for identity pedagogies as much as anti-identity teaching. And yet, what does the combination of these two strategies mean? Is such a combination envisioned as a union between feminist and lesbian and gay pedagogy (that is, identity pedagogies) and queer pedagogy (that is, "beyond identity" pedagogy)? If so, how would this union "look" in the classroom? Would feminist ideas, like feminist pedagogies, be relegated to being *only* essentializing and preoccupied with identity politics? Would this not vilify feminism in the process of asserting a queer move (Walters 1996)? Would, as Weed asks, "the feminism against which queer (pedagogy) defines itself [be] a feminism reduced to almost a caricature: a feminism tied to a concern for gender, bound to a regressive and monotonous binary opposition?" (1997, xi). How would one retain the feminist edge to teaching queerly?

TEACHING IN-BETWEEN IDENTITY AND ANTI-IDENTITY

Femiqueer Pedagogies

The issue of how to combine feminism and queer theory, or standpoint epistemologies and deconstructive ones, is in fact indicative of much larger questions concerning the relationship between feminist and queer theory/politics, and between lesbian/gay and queer studies. Theoretically, there are teachers/scholars who identify as "feminist theorists," "queer theorists," "queer feminist theorists," and "feminist queer theorists"—all of whom might participate in this discussion in very different ways. Some might see feminist and queer theories, for example, as engaging different projects; namely, analyzing gender, on the one hand, and sexuality, on the other. Others, such as

Butler, would argue that "politically, the costs are too great to choose between feminism, on the one hand, and radical sexual theory, on the other"
(1997, 18). Still others, as Weed points out, read queer theory as assuming
a "whiteness" that counters work about race and racialization in relation to
gender (1997, ix). In a similar way, lesbian and gay scholarship may be
viewed as centering on identities, while queer theory may be conceived as
disrupting them.

The introduction of sexual difference theories into pedagogical discussion is of great significance in that it offers a means of teaching queer lessons
concerning the complexity of sexual and gender identities, while it also
addresses the important grounding of sexuality studies in standpoint (identity) concerns. Sexual difference tactics allow for a more productive negotia-
tion of key challenges in the sexualities classroom—particularly, the persistence
of bodily materiality and the importance of identity work within such university spaces. In theoretical terms, both feminist sexual difference theory
and queer theory confound classic boundaries between sex and gender in
ways central to contemporary understandings of sexualities. As Jagose explains, queer theory "describes those gestures and analytical modes which
dramatize incoherence in the allegedly stable relations between chromosomal sex, gender, and sexual desire" (1997, 3). Sexual difference theories,
while each distinct, likewise complicate the assumed parallel between sex and
gender and attendant heterosexual desire. Assuming that bodies exist in-between
social construction and material constraint, sexual difference theories critique
two theoretically problematic alternatives: to articulate gender as simply the
social manifestation of chromosomal sex is to collapse the distinction between
sex and gender, but to radically detach sex from gender is to erroneously imply
no substantial relation between them. Thus, sexual difference theories offer a
nice parallel to the complications proposed by queer theory. At the same time,
sexual difference theories ground their frameworks—more than queer theory—
in an interrogation of bodies and corporeality.

Precisely as analyses of bodies, sexual difference theories provide a way
to expand central tenets of queer pedagogy. By offering theoretically grounded
ideas regarding the materiality of sex and sexualities, sexual difference theories directly address the stumbling block we continually face in teaching: the
tangible presence of instructor/student bodies in the classroom and the assumed mappings between sex/gender and sex/gender/sexuality vis-à-vis those
bodies. Sexual difference theories also offer possibilities for teaching ambiguity that nicely juggle the interplay between identity and anti-identity. Although queer discussions of pedagogy address the balance between the two
strategies, the implication remains that an ideal queer pedagogy would centrally focus on anti-identity teaching (rather than a philosophy of in-between
identity and anti-identity). Sexual difference theories, by contrast (as discussed
in previous chapters), foreground the in-between. Consequently, a sexual difference pedagogy allows one to address students' essentialist assumptions about

identities without appealing to a pure constructionism. It affords an examination of identity claims without a rejection of those claims altogether. In what follows, I offer examples of how one might attempt to combine various pedagogies in the lesbian and gay studies classroom—effectively teaching in-between feminism and queer theory, lesbian/gay and queer studies, and identity and anti-identity projects.

Paradoxical Identities

During a semester of lesbian and gay studies, I engage instructor and student bodies many times to highlight their paradoxical and contradictory "nature"—employing various classroom exercises and strategies to complicate assumptions about identities. The first example proceeds as follows:[6] I begin the semester by coming out to the class as lesbian. Later in the semester, I mention a heterosexual sexual experience involving a high school boyfriend. Given this aspect of my history, I ask, "Would you say that I am really *bisexual?*" In so doing, I raise the question of how sexual identity categories are constituted vis-à-vis the sex of the persons involved. The underlying (sometimes stated) question is whether a lesbian can sleep with a man (and still be a lesbian). At the end of chapter 4, this seemingly paradoxical state of affairs was raised as an example of how our usual formulations of identity might be disrupted. In this context, students think through these destabilizations in various ways. Some students want to dismiss the high school boyfriend because "that was a long time ago" and should not factor into my present identity. Others ask whether I have ever self-identified as bisexual—arguing that if I have not, then no matter what the circumstances, I am not bisexual. Still others think that I must be bisexual if the story about the boyfriend is true; or, they question how I can identify as lesbian at all if I am telling the truth. That is, students argue that sexual identity must map according to the sex of the partner—I am bisexual if I have had sex with males and females, I am lesbian only if I have had sex with other females. In this example, students are presented with complications involving sexual identities from within the very context of a coming out narrative. Consequently, I "identify," but I also make it difficult for students to shore up the category *lesbian* at the same time as I claim it.

As the semester continues, I further destabilize identity categories by challenging students to think of me as "gay" instead of as lesbian or bisexual. This strategy proceeds as follows. First, I relay a coming out instance in which I used the term *gay* rather than *lesbian*. I then ask the class, "If I identify as lesbian, but I came out to someone as gay, was I being untrue to myself in using a term with which I do not identify?" In so asking, I press students to consider different meanings of lesbian and gay. As students begin discussing the gendered meanings of these categories, I ask, "Could I identify as a gay man?" Generally, students respond that I could not identify as a gay man because, first of all, I am not a man. To this claim, I respond, "How do you know [that I'm not a man]?" Questioning how students can be sure that I am (or identify as) a woman helps to introduce transgender issues into the discussion. It prompts students to reflect on the fluidity of gender and gender presentation, as well as the assumption that "being a man" or "being a woman" is purely grounded in anatomy/biology. These questions get played out on my body as students ponder whether there really is a woman standing in front of their classroom. It also serves to again highlight, for students, how we rely on assumptions of the sex of participants as signifiers of sexual identity. In sum, I first identify or "come out" as lesbian and then disrupt assumed definitions by suggesting potential membership in other categories—"bisexual," "gay," "gay male," and "transgender." This strategy destabilizes students' assumptions about the exclusivity of sexual/gender categories, while it maintains the significance of identity work within the lesbian and gay studies classroom.

Another way to render such destabilizations is to focus on categories that students can easily see as residing in-between binaries. For instance, given student assumptions about those who have sex-reassignment surgery (SRS), bringing these lived experiences (in some of their manifestations) into the classroom helps students to understand the interplay between identity construction and constraint. For example, one semester, a colleague knew that a known transgender activist (Kate Bornstein) would be invited to campus as a guest speaker. Using Bornstein's (1994) *Gender Outlaw*, the colleague introduced the idea that sex/gender is a performed and fluid experience. She continued this discussion by having students complete the Gender Aptitude test in the beginning of Bornstein's (1997) *My Gender Workbook*. Yet, in order to confound the categories, it was important to introduce other understandings of transgender experience as well. Ideally, the colleague would have ended the semester with a transgender guest panel comprising varying and conflicting views about what it means to be transgender—that is, expressing positions of identity while multiplying and disrupting their meanings. Because the town in which my colleauge teaches does not have many out trans-activists, she opted to have students read excerpts from transsexual autobiography (for example, *In Search of Eve* by Anne Bolin, and "The 'Empire' Strikes Back: A PostTranssexual Manifesto" by Sandy Stone). These readings conveyed various ways in which transgender identities are experienced and understood—making it difficult for students to easily firm up the category.

In addition, I use Loren Cameron's (1996) self-portraits in *Body Alchemy* to push student understandings of the category *transgender*. Cameron's self-portraits, as discussed in chapter 4, depict the sexed body itself in a state of perpetually ambiguous transition. The portraits display a resistance and refusal to fit neatly within the categories *male* and *female*, since Cameron's body is shown to be anatomically located in-between these two categories.

In the case of Cameron, to reiterate, there is no male or female body; rather, "male" and "female" are themselves in a state of flux and fluidity. From within this context, it is an interesting question what happens to gender when it is mapped onto the ambiguously sexed body. This example reveals the importance of the body (sex) and its relation to gender, while it further complicates the body (or the category *sex*) itself. It displays how trans-experiences serve to unravel many of our assumptions about the relationship between sex/gender and sexuality, while it simultaneously highlights the category *transgender* for students learning it for the first time.

By incorporating multiple claims made about transgender identities by those who live them, we not only introduce ideas that have complicated lesbian and gay politics, we also create a space in which students come to view these experiences as residing in-between classic paradigms. Teaching the complexity of transgender experience is a particularly effective strategy since students are oftentimes just learning the term *transgender* and seeking to "define" transgender experience. Hence, students are both able to define the category and to see the complications involved in this very project.

In-Between Bodies

In addition to classroom strategies that highlight the paradox of identities, I employ techniques that create a space in-between identity and anti-identity. I strive to engage students in a constant interplay between identity and anti-identity in the everyday act of lesbian and gay studies teaching. The lesbian and gay studies classroom is a particularly relevant site for teaching in-between identity and anti-identity, since a central component of lesbian and gay studies concerns theoretical and political questions about the formation of individual and group identity, and the dissolution or complication thereof. The classroom, quite often, becomes a space framed by identity narratives. This circumstance is reflected in student remarks that either assert the centrality of sexual identity categories or that question them. For example, students often make statements such as the following which affirm identity categories:[7]

- Human beings think using categories. That's just the way it is. Humans *have* to organize their experiences by way of categories; otherwise, there would be total chaos.

- Harvey Milk was a brave, Jewish, gay man.

- Would you please tell us the definitions of "gay," "lesbian," "bi-sexual," and "transgender"?

At the same time, students also disaffirm identity categories with statements such as these:

- Categories are restricting. We should get rid of categories.

- "Black," "African American," "homosexual," "gay." . . . I just don't know what term people want me to use. It's all too confusing. They keep changing their minds. How are we supposed to know what to say? How are we supposed to keep from offending someone? One person wants "black," another wants "African American." . . . I think we should just forget about calling people anything.

Generally speaking, the examples that affirm identity reveal an investment in the notion of stable identities and orientations. These remarks display an appreciation of identity categories, although they also reveal an assumption that identities are simply "given." On the other hand, the examples that disaffirm identity suggest student skepticism regarding the very topic of identity and the use of identity categories at all. These comments show a liberal tendency to erase the significance of difference by disallowing the importance of identity.[8] Consequently, to foreground a pedagogy that emphasizes both narratives of identity and anti-identity is a way to theoretically address the identity politics of the lesbian and gay classroom—challenging students to consider the possibilities that reside in-between these seemingly oppositional narratives.

One way to teach students the complexity of identity categories is through a classroom exercise involving an assigned "queer" identity. This exercise operates as follows. Around the third week of class (a point at which students have somewhat settled in), students are assigned a "queer i.d." based on class material (for example, James Baldwin, Gloria Anzaldúa, Leslie Feinberg, etc.). One requirement of this exercise is that students cannot reveal their identities to anyone until a scheduled class session when the identities become public. Students are asked to research their assigned identities, to think about them, and to specifically reflect on what makes their identities "queer." Students then present their assigned identities to the class, explaining "themselves" in terms of queerness. Students are to be creative in revealing/sharing/performing their assigned identities, but all narratives must be formulated in the first person. This exercise highlights the fluidity of identity in the following way: Identities are assigned to students, their task being to assume the given identity. However, because students must determine precisely how their assigned identities are "queer," students must think about themselves in more fluid terms. This exercise is designed so that students puzzle over the sense in which their identities are granted but also contested; that is, the way in which identities are both formulated and open to disruption. Students "come out" as their queer i.d., while they precisely "queer" their coming out narrative.

Another more subtle way to highlight the in-between in the classroom is to move students between videos and video clips that students relate to (that is, that represent images "like me") versus ones that students don't relate to (that is, that depict people "not at all like me"). For straight students, the video experience is ideally one of fluctuating between thinking, "These gay people are just like me," and "These gay people are nothing like me." This movement may be called the sameness/difference interplay because it does not simply convey either sameness ("like me") or difference ("not like me") in the portrayal of LGBT life. Instead, the portrayal is more unsettled and ambiguous—demonstrating LGBT people as both the same as and different from straight folks. There is an additional identity/anti-identity aspect to this strategy, since some of the videos are more grounded in an identity politic (for example, *Why Am I Gay?: Stories of Coming Out in America*), while others are more readily queer (for example, *Paris Is Burning*). Thus, lesbian and gay studies students are simultaneously situated in-between identities and anti-identities, sameness and difference. The challenge is to engage the identity narratives already existing within a lesbian and gay studies classroom in a way that allows students to see that they neither simply need to affirm the existence of core sexual/gender identities nor attest to their insignificance. The hope is that by keeping a constant interplay between considerations of identity and anti-identity, students come to understand the complexities involved in LGBT experiences.

Offering the sort of classroom climate outlined above plays into student assumptions that "bodies matter"[9] and that "identity" is significant, while it also takes seriously student declarations that categories are restricting and problematic. Thus, students are unable to leave the class simply avowing or disavowing sexual/gender identity. Rather, they are able to articulate the region in-between identity and anti-identity, as illustrated by the following statements:

- Madonna has said that she considers herself a gay man in a woman's body.

- Since Anne is now married to a man, and since she was only involved with one woman [Ellen], does that mean that she had "Ellen-specific lesbianism"?

Statements such as these can be read as reflecting both identity avowal and disavowal, while being neither simply identity claims nor anti-identity ones. Notably, these techniques for moving students back and forth between considerations of identity and anti-identity are accompanied by course materials and lectures that complicate their considerations of the interplay. Using readings from *Social Perspectives in Lesbian and Gay Studies* (1998) and *The Lesbian and Gay Studies Reader* (1993) helps to highlight both the creation of lesbian and gay identities, as well as "analyses that trace the operation of homosexuality in dominant codes and conventions of straight society"

(Seidman 1994, 176). Students thereby learn the identity lessons of lesbian and gay studies, while they experience the deconstruction of these lessons more in keeping with queer studies. The result is a classroom that highlights the complex position of lesbian and gay studies today—a position not reducible to teaching only about identity or anti-identity, standpoint or deconstructive perspectives, feminist or queer ideas.

FINAL THOUGHTS ON FEMIQUEER PEDAGOGIES

> For those of us who work in the interstices of the relation between queer theory and feminism (as well as other contemporary critical discourses), and who insist on continuing the important intellectual tradition of immanent critique, the risk will always take the following form: if one analyzes the heterosexist assumptions of feminist theory, one will be construed as "anti-" or "post-" feminist; if one analyzes the anti-feminism of some gay and lesbian theory, one will be construed as hostile to that lesbian and gay theory.
>
> —Butler in Weed and Schor 1997

In this chapter, I have argued for the importance of teaching at the interstices between identity and anti-identity. I have argued for a student involvement in the identity/anti-identity project very much in keeping with feminist pedagogy. The value of incorporating various pedagogies has been suggested by Rothenberg (1998), in her discussion of using both multicultural and antiracist pedagogies to teach about race/class/gender, and by Pelligrini and Franklin (1996), in their discussion of teaching from both a lesbian feminist and a queer camp perspective. Using multiple classroom pedagogies has been understood as a way to better teach the complexities of theoretical material—an important point for the teaching of lesbian and gay studies. Teaching lesbian and gay studies without engaging the identity narratives that characterize the classroom risks reproducing what Seidman calls "the arcane polemics between constructionists and essentialists" (Seidman 1994, 109). In addition, queerly teaching identity and anti-identity, when feminist pedagogies are often identity/standpoint-based, risks reducing feminist ideas to mere caricatures of identity. Instead, using feminist and lesbian/gay ideas, in conjunction with ones from queer theory, allows for more successful teaching of the theoretically and politically complex relationship between feminist and queer, lesbian/gay and queer, identity and anti-identity, standpoint and deconstruction. Indeed, to teach in the space in-between these contested categories and positions is to teach in a way that keeps with sexual difference theories. It is to teach in a way that highlights in-between bodies—student bodies, instructor bodies, the lived bodies of those "studied." In this way, adopting strategies that expand teaching between identity and anti-identity offers a means to retain the feminist/lesbian/gay edge to teaching queer lessons.

CHAPTER SIX

THE TROUBLE WITH "QUEER"

The play between feminine and masculine elements that we contain in heterosexist eyes; the parody of masculine/feminine, the play with illusion that transgresses boundaries; the rejection of masculine/feminine in our self-understanding that some of us make our mark; all contain a rejection of purity.

—Lugones 1996

The life project of "queer," although it holds possibilities for anarchic and inventive identities, is too often used as a bludgeon, robbing authentic vital transsexual life experiences of their unique intelligence. I have been asked if I'm "queer," and I'm never sure how to answer. Although I am definitely a "freak," and therefore a member of the general "queer" family of perverts, I am also heterosexual and appear to be relatively gender role congruent as a male.

—Valerio 2002

TRANS-INVISIBILITY REVISITED

In chapter 4, I raised the issue of trans-"treatment," noting the murderer and the psychiatric institution as two remarkable sites. Common to both of these sites, I suggested, is a refusal to tolerate in-between bodies and nonnormative sex-gender mappings. This repudiation of the atypical results in efforts to either outright obliterate (through murder) or remake (through psychiatric intervention) the trans-person. In this regard, such efforts can be considered—minimally—attempts to render trans-identities invisible. I have argued that insofar as sexual difference theories do not explicitly consider trans-experiences or foreground instances of more than two clear sexes (even if "the sexes" have been opened to reinterpretation), sexual difference theories are likewise implicated in trans-invisibility. Nonetheless, as I highlighted

83

in chapter 5, a strength of sexual difference theories is their usefulness in reconfiguring identities. In terms of sexualities pedagogy, this means that sexual difference theories offer a way to utilize feminist pedagogy and queer pedagogy in one classroom space. A sexual difference pedagogy (that is, a "femiqueer" pedagogy) is positioned in-between the feminist and lesbian/gay standpoints of identity pedagogies and the queer challenge posed by anti-identity ones.

In what follows, I wish to revisit the issue of trans-invisibility. Here, however, I wish to consider trans-invisibility from within a discussion of trans-exclusion[1] from lesbian and gay politics, on the one hand, and from the concept of "queerness," on the other hand. That is, trans-experiences (especially trans*sexual* experiences) can be positioned in-between lesbian/gay and queer political positions, often resulting in the inclusion in neither. While I do not focus on sexual difference theories explicitly in this discussion, I maintain that the positions of transsexual activists highlighted here are consistent with sexual difference theory's emphasis on bodily materiality and the grounded "nature" of the lived body. In other words, these activists warn of the dangers of identities construed as overly fluid and lacking grounding. They ask what their place might be within discussions informed by a somewhat rigid lesbian/gay politics, on the one hand, and a sweeping queer politics, on the other hand.

Jerry Falwell and Tinky Winky

In considering the general issue of trans-invisibility, I have found myself recalling the rather well-known "readings"—several years ago—of Tinky Winky (from the children's television show *Teletubbies*) and Ernie and Bert (from the program *Sesame Street*) as a "homosexual" and as a "homosexual couple" respectively. These "readings" came from Jerry Falwell—a professed straight man—who claimed to know the status of Tinky Winky and Ernie and Bert vis-à-vis their sexualities. A rather interesting aspect of the Falwell incident, at the time, was the following: To the best of my knowledge, queer communities had not considered the sexualities of Tinky Winky (or of Ernie and Bert) until Falwell claimed to know their sexualities, and relatedly, found it necessary to share this perceived dangerous fact with the nation. I remember hearing self-identified queer individuals ridicule Falwell for actually spending time and energy contemplating the sexualities of televised cartoon-show characters and Muppets. However, at the same time that they maintained Falwell's claims as absurd, queer folks embraced Tinky Winky as "one of their own." Tinky Winky became a bona fide member of queer communities, and an addition to queer households, as queer novelty shops and e-businesses stocked Tinky Winky merchandise and local department stores ran out of Tinky Winky-ware (dolls, key chains, and the like) even as other *Teletubbies* characters remained on store shelves. Through the Falwell incident, Tinky Winky was catapulted to (queer) stardom.

What an interesting route to a queer identity: from an uncontemplated television character, to a named and dangerous homosexual presence, to an embraced member of queer communities at large. This conferring of "queer" status on Tinky Winky is, in some sense, the antithesis of a self-identity claim. That is, Tinky Winky has never said, "I am queer," or, "I am gay." Of course, Falwell *thinks* that Tinky Winky's color (purple) and his accessories (his purse) make these claims very clearly; Tinky Winky need not utter the actual words. It is worth noting, however, that Falwell's assessment of Tinky Winky also follows a curious path: he first assigns Tinky Winky a sex (male), then assesses that sex (by reading the color and the accessory as "inappropriate" gender attributions for a male), and then conflates gender and sexuality (by labeling Tinky Winky a "homosexual" on the basis of these "inappropriate" gender characteristics). This line of thinking follows the traditional trajectory discussed earlier in this book and again highlights the fact that different sex-gender mappings do not yield the same meanings. If Falwell had designated Tinky Winky as female, for instance, then concern over Tinky Winky's purse and color would have been unlikely. In the present case, it could be that Tinky Winky's triangle head-piece clinched the "homosexual" assessment for Falwell, although this inference additionally represents a curious course, for: (1) who has actually ever seen such an antenna-like piece of gay pride-ware?, and (2) do *all* triangles then become queer-suspects simply in virtue of their being triangles?

In a significant way, however, the act of conferring queer status on Tinky Winky via Falwell, on the part of queer communities, *can* be seen as a self-identity movement—if not by Tinky Winky as an individual, then by queer communities as collectives. That is, if identifying *oneself* has such force given a history of labeling by others (for example, religious and medical institutions), then claiming Tinky Winky—in a sense *from* Falwell—is a similar act of self-identification. Through purchasing their own Tinky Winkys and displaying them proudly, they transformed Tinky Winky from dangerous, sick, and perverted Tinky Winky to "you go girl!" Tinky Winky; from outed "homosexual" Tinky Winky to "queer-with-a-cause" Tinky Winky.

If it is absurd to ruminate on the sexualities of cartoon-show characters, then one might ask: Why did queer communities embrace Tinky Winky?, and, Why did they engage with this absurdity? I think that the account above works to explain the response of queer communities in the following way. The response effectively says: "Yes, Jerry Falwell, Tinky Winky *is* a raving queer. And we are claiming Tinky Winky. He is ours. In fact, we are taking him from you, and we will buy so many Tinky Winkys that you will never get rid of him!" Rather than try to prove Falwell wrong in his assessment of Tinky Winky (for example, by explaining how Falwell actually ascribes a sex, then reads gender attributes as inappropriate for that sex, and then conflates gender and sexuality to render Tinky Winky a "homosexual"), the overwhelming response on the part of queer communities was simply to

buy as many Tinky Winkys as possible. Such consumer-oriented activism
could be examined, in another space, in relation to a "queer" history of
boycotting homophobic businesses and patronizing queer-friendly ones—
notable examples being the Coors beer boycott, on the one hand, and the
Advocate's list of gay-friendly companies (Subaru and Bank of America, for
instance), on the other hand.

Trans Erasure

For the chapter at hand, I would like to draw attention to the fact that the
dominant response to the Tinky Winky/Falwell incident—that is, the dominant gay male and lesbian discourse—failed to highlight Tinky Winky's
potential *gender* transgression in favor of an emphasis on Tinky Winky's
sexuality. Rather than identify Tinky Winky in "his" possible transness (and
not necessarily gayness), effectively meant an erasure of trans-identity within
queer communities' adoptions of "him." Patrick Califia remarks, in his preface to the second edition of *Sex Changes: Transgender Politics*, that
"[t]ransgendered people are virtually invisible within mass media, or appear
only as characters in story lines that bolster transphobia" (2003, xxix). Keeping with Califia, a rendering of Tinky Winky as "gay," on the part of queer
communities themselves, can be seen to effect a twofold invisibility. In other
words: (1) transgendered people—real or fictional—are routinely marginalized
within mainstream media, and (2) labeling Tinky Winky as gay and not
trans serves to reinforce this invisibility. As a serious example of trans-erasure
being reinscribed by gay male and lesbian communities is "the murder of
army private first class Barry Winchell, who was killed by soldiers in his unit
who were incensed about the fact that he was dating a preoperative transsexual woman, Calpernia Sarah Addams" (Califia 2003, xxxii). According to
Califia, "Addams was pressured into downplaying her status as a transsexual
woman by gay rights organizations that wanted to publicize the Winchell
case as an example of homophobia in the military" (2003, xxxii). During this
process, and as a further instance of transphobia itself, Addams was referred
to as "an inconvenient woman" (xxxii).

These two cases, one involving a children's television character and
the other a murdered soldier and his partner involve two varieties of trans-
invisibility: in the first case, an instance of trans-identity not being seen or
appreciated due to its conflation with gayness (that is, the merging of gender
and sexuality), and in the second case, an instance of trans-identity being
purposely marginalized, or we could say *re*-marginalized, in order to *favor*
gayness (that is, drawing attention toward homophobia, and away from transphobia). These two forms of trans-erasure likewise follow a traditional line
of thought, discussed earlier in this project. Here, in the present two cases,
trans-identities are either collapsed into gay identities (gender and sexuality
become one) or trans-identities are detached from gay identities (gender is

subordinated to sexuality). In neither instance, it could be argued, are trans-identities granted visibility or voice on their own terms.

An additional example of trans-invisibility that I would like to offer here is one in which trans-identity is precisely targeted by homophobia due to the very conflation of transness and gayness. This example occurs in the film *Ma vie en rose* (*My Life In Pink*), directed by Alain Berliner. In the film, the main character, Ludo, is labeled "bent" (homosexual) because he likes boys (specifically, his classmate Jerome). However, Ludo does not consider himself to be a boy; instead, he conceives himself to be a girl. Ludo says, though no one really seems to hear him, that he will marry Jerome when he grows up and becomes a girl. Not recognizing this qualification, Ludo's mother tells him that "boys do not marry other boys—or, [they do so] only rarely," to which Ludo replies, "I know that."

Thus, it can be asked whether Ludo *is* gay. Based on the information we receive in the film, it seems likely that Ludo is *not* gay; rather, Ludo is more probably transgender. In fact, if Ludo transitions from male to female when he grows up, and if he marries a man, then Ludo will be part of a straight couple. In this event, if Ludo remains exclusively interested in men, then he will most likely consider himself to be a straight woman. Ludo would represent the (fictional) counterpart to (real-life) Max Wolf Valerio, quoted in the opening epigraph to this chapter, who transitioned from female to male and considers himself to be a straight man. Thus, it is somewhat ironic that Ludo is taken to be gay (or, at least, on the path to a gay identity) and is targeted with repeated homophobic attacks during the course of the film. Ludo is also put through many attempts at "treatment" which are reminiscent of Scholinski's experience in a psychiatric ward: cutting his hair, demanding that he wear "boy's clothes" and play soccer, taking him to the psychologist, allowing him to wear a skirt in order to defuse the taboo, and threatening him with a fly swatter, to name a few.

It could also be mentioned that Ludo's transness may again be rendered invisible in the possible scenario outlined above, in which Ludo grows up and identifies as a straight woman. That is to say, insofar as Ludo (or any biological male) transitions and lives as a woman, or any biological female transitions and lives as a man, it is often the case that this person is precisely *not* seen as trans. Rather, the person is often seen only as a woman or a man. Trans-identity, as contrasted with gender congruent identity, is again erased through a process in which perception grounds the identity category into which the person is placed. Jason Cromwell makes this point, in *Transmen and FTMs*, when he remarks that "[m]any female-bodied transpeople are or become invisible by living as men. They often become invisible as transgendered people and only visible as men" (1999, 12).

Consequently, part of the project of many in the transgender movement is to reclaim visibility and identity as trans-people—thereby refusing to participate in the expected full assimilation into categories of "man" or "woman." Such assimilation would require a disconnection from one's trans-past or trans-history. Califia comments:

> In truth I don't know—and may never know—what it's like to be
> a man. I will probably always be a female-to-male transsexual who
> passes. To hit this brick wall every day is to raise the question, do
> I wish I had been born male? If I could eradicate every trace of my
> transsexuality and live completely as a man, would I do it? I know
> that many transsexuals would say yes, in a heartbeat. But I continue
> to see something valuable in being perched on the Great Gender
> Divide. (2003, xiii)

For Califia, recognition that the female-to-male transsexual is never "simply" a man marks an awareness of one's trans-past—a past that still informs one's present. For some, the physical scars of sex reassignment surgery, as mentioned in chapter 4, are claimed as sources of pride that link bodily past and present. Even with such self-initiated efforts to maintain trans-identity, however, there remains the possibility that one's identity will be collapsed into clear "man" or "woman" categories by others.

QUEERNESS, HETEROSEXISM, HOMOPHOBIA

To briefly return to the Tinky Winky/Falwell affair, I think it is also significant to point out that at the time of the Falwell claim, some queer individuals argued that cartoon characters do not have sexualities. Hence, in musing over children's programming, Falwell had simply gone too far. This was a case, some argued, of homophobia run rampant. But is it really true that cartoon characters do not have sexualities, and how did Falwell see Tinky Winky as so obviously male and so clearly "homosexual"?

Regarding the first question, it seems fairly undeniable that cartoon characters certainly *do* have sexualities, which is to say, they have *hetero*sexualities.[2] Despite a tenuous relevance, or an outright irrelevance, to their story lines, heterosexuality (in the form of heterosexual relationships, or heterosexually oriented banter) pervades most films for children. In fact, if there is a purpose to these seemingly pointless scenes, the aim could be taken to be the socialization of children into a life of heterosexuality. Concerning the second question, given depictions of cartoon heterosexuality enmeshed within the story lines of films for children, it is interesting to ask what happens when a cast of characters (for instance, the *Teletubbies*) is presented who are neither clearly gendered nor sexually obvious. It seems reasonable to maintain that given a heterosexist lens—through which *no* sexuality is generally seen, when an argument could be made for glaring *hetero*sexuality—Tinky Winky becomes marked in ways demonstrating a shift in representation. That is, owing to the fact that heterosexuality is normative, depictions of it often go unnoticed;

however, when the typical heterosexualized frame changes, representations become marked precisely in virtue of their being nonnormative. Tinky Winky is easily designated as a "homosexual" since "he" somehow does not fit the standard (heterosexual) story line. Ernie and Bert are likewise interpreted as lovers, I would imagine, since their male-male coupling occurs within a typical and unacknowledged heterosexual space.

Moreover, claims regarding a purported asexuality of cartoon characters are also informed by—and operate through—a similar heterosexist lens. In other words, while they maintain no sexuality, there appears to be—in point of fact—clear heterosexuality. The paradox of this state of affairs for queer communities can be seen if we consider that queer readings (of texts and other representations) are often premised on the idea of noting "queerness" between the lines of mainstream productions. This means that queer readings purportedly unbalance the everyday heteronormative frame through unveiling queerness residing within it; thus, Falwell's reading of Tinky Winky could be considered much more queer than the claim that cartoon characters have no sexualities. In fact, I would argue that while Falwell's interpretation of Tinky Winky may simply be considered homophobic and not queer (indeed, Falwell's rendering of Tinky Winky was introduced in this chapter as "traditional"), insofar as Falwell nonetheless gathers symbols and translates them to render a "gay" Tinky Winky, he could be viewed as employing central tenets of queer theory/methodology (which is not to say that he does so purposefully). I think that this possibility, which represents a paradox turned back on queer communities, so to speak, signals a danger in an overreliance on or an overinvestment in the concept of "queer" or "queerness." In other words, once Jerry Falwell succeeds in offering—for all intents and purposes—a queer reading, I think it is sensible to ask how well "queer" is serving LGBT communities. How often do homophobic renderings and queer ones actually look the same?

Questions Concerning "Queer"

Even if the idea of Falwell offering a queer reading is not persuasive to the reader, we might nonetheless ask the following series of questions regarding the term *queer* and its deployment: Have the borders of queer, at least in certain contexts, become too expansive? Has the explosion of boundaries enabled by queer helped (or hindered) working against concrete forms of lesbian/gay/bisexual/transgender discrimination and oppression? Has the notion of queer tended to "float off into postmodern space," to re-quote Zita from chapter 4 of the present work. Has queer become disconnected from the material conditions and historical circumstances of a variety of lives? Has the concept of queerness allowed the entrance of "outsiders" who have, at times, co-opted or derailed community agendas?

While the queer concept was certainly employed to do positive work—countering a static identity politic by providing space for a more inclusive and expansive vision, and challenging sexuality conceived only in terms of mutual exclusion—I wonder at what cost the movement away from identity categories in favor of queerness has come? Has the deployment of queer failed to be subversive, in many instances, and merely been at the disposal of rather mainstream interests (for example, the use of "queer" on network and cable television, as in *Queer Eye for the Straight Guy* or *Queer as Folk*)? Has the term *queer* become (too) assimilated into dominant society/culture? Valerio raises a set of concerns that can be attached to these questions. He contends:

> The conflation of genderfuck into the transmovement has confused and eroded authentic transsexual voices. Although there's nothing inherently wrong with gender-bending, gender-fuck, and the assorted hyphenated identities becoming common in the queer world, I must ask: What does it really have to do with my life? The answer is, increasingly, nothing. (2002, 249)

With this statement, Valerio raises the issue of how useful queer is to his lived identity. Not only does Valerio consider queer to have little use to him, he also indicates that his transsexual identity has been diluted through its association with queerness. He suggests that emphasizing fluidity and queerness has actually worked to conceal and tear at his life as a transsexual man. Califia makes a somewhat different point in remarking:

> While it is certainly true that some transgendered people do not see themselves as members of the queer community and a tiny number may even be actively homophobic, it is also true that the very existence of gay and bisexual transmen and women continues to be controversial, and our participation in lesbian and gay male communities is often contested. (2003, xxxiv)

Califia's comment points back to concerns about trans-invisibility within gay and lesbian politics. Here, Califia indicates that transgendered people are often marginalized within so-called queer communities themselves.

Reconsidering Terminology

Within the context of questions over "queer" and "queerness," we might consider the return of many Native Americans to the term *Indian* and many African Americans to the term *black* (though the origins of these terms are not analogous). We might ask whether "queers" should follow a similar gesture. For instance, Sherman Alexie and others have maintained that Native American is too inclusive a term since anyone born in the United States can claim to be a *Native* American. Similarly, given that a white South African who moves to the United States might claim to be an *African* American, as suggested in chapter 3, the result may be an unwelcome erasure of *black* American identity through the blurring of this label. As a white philosophy student recently remarked:

> Mister Dave Matthews of the Dave Matthews Band should be able to say, uncontestedly, that he is an African American because he was born and raised in South Africa but now lives in the U.S. That is what makes an African American in my opinion, the *born* in Africa part.

Of course, a number of points could be made in response to this comment. For instance, this remark, while provocative, fails to register the desire of many black Americans to claim the term *African American* since, in the words of Johnny Washington, it "heightens among the people of the African Diaspora the sense of affinity between themselves and the people on the continent of Africa" (Washington 1993, 57). Also, the example of Dave Matthews misses a significant point about power and privilege. As Paul Kivel contends in *Uprooting Racism*:

> If, when you move down the streets of major cities, other people assume, based on skin color, dress, physical appearance, or total impression, that you are white, then in American society that counts for being white. (2002, 9)

Consequently, the lived experiences of (white) Dave Matthews and those of many black Americans differ radically, and these experiential differences reflect different construals of whiteness and blackness within the United States.

The Dave Matthews example is also significant in considering trans-experiences in that it connects identity to "birth." In the view of my student, a "genuine" African American person must be born in Africa. Likewise, in a remark concerning transsexual experiences, Cromwell argues that:

> Discourses such as anthropology, history, medicine, and pyschology, as well as some feminist interpretations of these discourses, render lives invisible by arguing that FTMs and transmen are "really" and "truly" women because the "truth" is in their female bodies. (1999, 11)

In other words, based on the Dave Matthews logic of my student (if my student were to hold analogous logic on matters of race and gender), it would be difficult to ever admit a genetic male as a woman—whether the genetic male had undergone surgical reconstruction or not. I think that this point concerning birth adds a complication to Kivel's contention that what counts as white in the United States is being perceived as white, since in the case

of racial passing being "found out" has been a source of extreme danger, as
noted in chapter 3. Similarly, being found out as trans (and not simply a
genetic male or female) is a source—perhaps the paradigmatic source—of
anti-trans violence and discrimination. It could be said that while being
perceived as a man or woman has much to do with who "counts" as a man
or woman in the United States, the appeal to perception comes with a
caveat: that if one's body-of-birth is found to run counter to one's gender
presentation, then the body (the so-called underlying truth) appears to over-
ride that perception.

ALPHABET SOUP

While the LGBT movement has never completely done away—at any given
moment—with the identity terms *lesbian, gay, bisexual,* or *transgender,* I wonder whether a more concrete return to these (or similar) labels should be
initiated. To ask this question is not to imply a retreat to an uncomplicated
identity politic. Rather, the following point by Iris Marion Young (articulated here by Lugones) is crucial. Lugones relays that "Young sees group
representation as necessary because she thinks differences are irreducible:
'People from one perspective can never completely understand and adopt the
point of view of those with other group-based perspectives and histories' "
(1998, 121). Regarding the issue of group identities, Lugones herself asserts:

> The affiliative histories include the formation of voices in contesta-
> tion that reveal the enmeshing of race, gender, culture, class, and
> other differences that affect and constitute the identity of the group's
> members. This is a very significant difference in direction from the
> one suggested by postmodern literature, which goes against a poli-
> tics of identity and toward minimizing the political significance of
> groups. (1996, 292)

So, again, I wonder whether queer communities should move away from
emphasizing queerness to embracing more complicated politics of identity
such as those formulated by Young and Lugones. To do so would mean
incorporating concerns by trans-people, such as Valerio and Califia, that the
term *queer* is too amorphous to genuinely include them and that the *queer*
label is not as inclusive in practice as it is purported to be in theory.

The string-of-letters phenomenon, or "alphabet soup," is likewise problematic for trans-people, since trans-identities—as gender identities and not
necessarily sexual minority identities—are marginalized within the lettering
sequence. According to Califia:

> Unfortunately, despite the common use of the acronym GLBT,
> transgendered activists cannot count on the help of feminists or gay

activists, even when common cause could easily be made around issues like antiviolence work or civil rights legislation. In 2000, *Out* magazine actually dared to distribute a "survey" (actually an ad for new subscribers) asking, "Should transgenders be a part of the gay rights movement? (check yes or no box)." (2003, xxxii–iii)

Califia's comment points to two further issues. First, his use of "common cause" suggests that the string-of-letters—if they remain intact—must function more as a coalition and less as a soup. That is, the integrity of each letter (and the life experience that each position represents) must be maintained, rather than lost, in pursuit of common ends. And second, the simple fact of *Out* magazine's survey tells us a great deal about issues of power and privilege within the string-of-letters itself. In other words, if some letters are positioned in ways that afford a genuine questioning of other letters' inclusion, then this suggests that not all letters in the sequence maintain equal positions of power and privilege. This dissymmetry conflicts with the very intention and implication of the letters which is to afford equality to each member of the group.

Finally, an additional concern involving the string-of-letters might be briefly noted here, which is that the proliferation of letters used to designate gender and sexual minority communities ("L," "G," "B," and "T"—often with an "A" [allied] perhaps with a "Q" [queer], sometimes with two "Qs" [queer and questioning], and maybe with an "I" [intersex]) presents an interchangeability problem in a number of contexts. That is to say, the "G" is all too easily substituted for the "L," or the "L" exchanged for the "B," or the "T" traded for the "LGB," or the "A" swapped for "LGBT" experience. The letters within the LGBTAQQI sequence have been clumped together in a way that readily affords an interchange between and among them.[3] One way that this difficulty manifests itself is in cases where selecting one—any one—of the letters in the string is thought to accomplish group representation. However, we can see the problem with such a collapse of the letters in the string into one if we adopt the sort of frame suggested by Young and Lugones (again, one in which each letter marks an irreducible experience). I would argue that when the swapping and/or collapse of letters occurs, it more often than not favors the more privileged members of the group—as suggested by the *Out* magazine survey highlighted by Califia—and works against (or renders invisible) those with the least power. With this point in mind, I would like to close with a final comment by Valerio on the issue of privilege. Valerio's remark underscores the idea that trans-erasure is not simply an invisibility in relation to mainstream society, but that trans-invisibility is maintained as an integral component of queer/LGB communities themselves. Valerio states:

> [I often experience what can be described as] the loss of *nontranssexual privilege*. The sudden discovery that I'm a bona fide weirdo who's

had a sex change could toss me right out of the category "member
of the human race." Nontranssexuals have the privilege of taking
their gender for granted. They don't live in the constant insecurity
that they might be discovered and therefore have their gender identity discounted and stolen from them. (2002, 248)

Thus, while Valerio is often challenged on his position as "straight man,"
afforded through surgical reconstruction, he emphasizes that matters of privilege are not so easy to specify. Like Califia, Valerio may be more accurately
described as "passing," for if his bodily history were to be discovered, it would
become apparent that the "body of birth" is highly relevant to the evalua-
tions of many. That is to say, "man" mapped onto "genetic female" renders
a different meaning than "man" mapped onto "genetic male." Hence, Valerio
and others arguably reside in a space in-between the granted and adopted—
a space not easily reified as a position of political power.

CONCLUSION

RECONFIGURED IDENTITIES

Human existence and identity are not simply given. To become human and develop a human identity is a process of invention (self invention), of personal and collective action conditioned by social relations. Oppression robs people of their identities and imposes rigid stultifying identities on its victims.

—Birt 1998

They would chop me up into little fragments and tag each piece with a label. You say my name is ambivalence? Think of me as . . . a many armed and legged body with one foot on brown soil, one on white, one in straight society, one in the gay world, another in the working class, the socialist, and the occult worlds. Who, me confused? Ambivalent? Not so. Only your labels split me.

—Anzaldúa 1983

By way of conclusion, it can be said that sexual difference theories partici-pate in efforts to reconfigure identities. Although sexual difference theories do not explicitly address many of the possibilities for identities examined here, my investigation of these bodies and identities nonetheless takes sexual difference theory as a point of departure. While sexual difference theories do not conceive of identities as simply given or static, neither do they imply that identities are open to limitless instantiations. Rather, identities must be materially grounded even as they are (re)negotiated by the subject. In the process, "the subject" itself is constituted. Thus, "the subject" is rendered in a state of becoming—lived in-between nature and culture, in-between what is given and what is assumed.

For Irigaray, of fundamental concern is the issue of sexual difference or the category *woman*. Given that sexual difference has been rendered invisible within Western frameworks, in Irigaray's view, "woman" has never been a subject. Thus, her being—even as a becoming—has been denied her. We could perhaps say that women as individuals cannot be subjects if "woman" in general has been denied subjectivity. At the same time, there is reason to suspect the notion of " 'woman' in general," as this "woman" is likely premised on a white, heterosexual model. As *lived*, for instance, there is no generalized "woman." An emphasis on sexual difference, by Irigaray and sexual difference theories more broadly, has clearly neglected intersections between "sexual difference" and other social markers. As a result, and no matter how productive these theories might be for rethinking the relationship between sex and gender, the theories nonetheless fail to escape a white frame of reference.

One might argue that Irigaray's emphasis on sexual difference as a foundational difference points to her connection with psychoanalytic discourse. For instance, her focus on sexual difference might be explained by her interest in the little boy's and the little girl's entries into the symbolic order; that is, in how their respective relationships to language position them differently. I have emphasized Irigaray's engagement with the Western philosophical, rather than psychoanalytic, tradition due to its focus on binary thinking and Irigaray's call to reconsider the basic categories of reality. I have highlighted Irigaray's claim that social/political progress will not be successful prior to a more basic shift in our primary organizing categories. As support for this claim, Irigaray indicates the erosion of gains won by women and feminist concentration on "critical demands."

Concerning race, I have maintained that sexual difference theorists have excluded race from their reconception of bodies. This exclusion is demonstrated, in Irigaray's work, through her emphasis on the ontological nature of sexual difference. I have emphasized the fact that the notion of "sexual difference" employed by sexual difference theory is effectively taken to be an unmarked category when it is more likely marked as white. Having said this, certain insights of sexual difference theory, including Gatens's notion of contingency, are significant for the way they reconsider the relations between categories. For Gatens, different mappings of sex to gender do not render the same meanings. Thus, Gatens shifts feminist focus from the category *gender* to the category *sex*, suggesting that the body is never neutral and the relation between gender and sex is of central theoretical (and practical) importance. I have suggested that a notion of "contingency" can be found in the work of several race theorists and literary authors. The idea that different connections between raced bodies and raced cultures yield different meanings offers a model for rethinking race, implying (among other things) that "to be raced" is as much a matter of becoming as being. Given that mappings of lightness to white bodies and lightness to black bodies do not render the same meanings, and that mappings of darkness to white bodies and darkness to black bodies do not provide the same significances, these different "outcomes" indicate a *normative* aspect to the category *race*. "Racial mixing" can be offered as a different example of this phenomenon through which white/ white and black/black mappings have been demanded and sanctions against the mixing of the races have been imposed (legal and otherwise).

In this regard, we can consider other situations in which mappings do not conform, in a traditional way, to lived experiences. Transgender identities, for instance, precisely demonstrate the deceit of a naturalized sex-gender system. While gender is taken to be the natural outgrowth of biological sex, trans-bodies demonstrate that unexpected sex-gender combinations are quite possible. Indeed, nonnormative mappings are lived by various individuals on a daily basis. However, despite being lived, the fact that certain connections between sex and gender are not socially sanctioned is evidenced by instances of trans-violence and trans-"treatment." I have claimed that even though sexual difference theorists have rethought the relationship between sex and gender, it can still be asked whether sexual difference theories are sufficiently nuanced to address trans-identities. That is, even though trans-identities would nicely fit within the discussion initiated by sexual difference theorizing, they are nonetheless excluded from that theoretical endeavor itself.

Despite exclusions by sexual difference theories, the frameworks they offer nonetheless extend significant benefits. I have used the example of the sexualities classroom, maintaining that theories of sexual difference can productively ground a pedagogy that lies in-between standpoint and deconstruction, feminist/LGBT pedagogy and queer pedagogy. With respect to identities and bodies, this means neither reifying identities nor renouncing them; it means attending to [lived] bodies and opening the terrain of theoretical/experiential possibilities. Theories of sexual difference imply strategies and politics that highlight in-between bodies and positions. Advocated is neither an unconsidered assumption of identities nor an outright erasure of them; advanced is a multiplicity of identities and a grounding for this proliferation.

One problem with an expansion of identity categories (such as that enabled by the concept of "queer") is that some individuals feel excluded from articulations of identities as free-floating (as demonstrated by the idea that "everyone is a little queer/ trans"). These individuals argue that material aspects of identity are not adequately addressed when identity labels (rendered as "fluid") are applied too broadly. Ironically, this claim indicates that the purported inclusive deployment of these terms actually fosters further exclusions. Rather than maintaining a "reification" of identity (as Valerio's reference to "authentic transsexual experience" might imply), I have proposed that many transsexual individuals stress an in-betweenness that undermines traditional notions of authenticity. This in-betweenness resides in bodies through the idea that one's trans-body always leaves a trace, or residue, or reminder. Consequently, one can never "fully" or "entirely" be a man or a woman post surgical reassignment. This insight is illustrated by the recognition of the danger that transsexual individuals face if they are ever "found out." In more positive terms, the embrace of surgical sex reassignment scars demonstrates this remainder. I have suggested that these scars also gesture back to the discussion of the navel in the present project. Through Irigaray, I have proposed the navel as an ambiguous site, representing both a point of connection to the mother and a mark of detachment from her. The navel and the surgical scar link bodily past and present—indicating that the past is never fully "overcome"; rather, the "past" resides within one's "present." At the same time, one is never fully immersed or trapped within a past, since assumptions of identity evolve through and despite that past. That is to say, identities themselves are always in states of becoming (as well as of being).

The issue of self-identity emerges as an outgrowth of considering sexual difference theories (though the concept is not exclusive to them). Since sexual difference frameworks both open space for renegotiations of identities and seek to anchor these identities within material circumstances, the reconfigured identities of sexual difference theory are neither static nor free-floating. Indeed, the anchor may serve as an appropriate metaphor for the identities enabled by sexual difference theories insofar as a vessel that is anchored is both "grounded" and free to flow—free to flow, that is, within the constraints afforded by the anchor. Consequently, there is "space," on sexual difference accounts, for identities such as those offered by Babe or Ludo. Babe, a natural-born pig, considers himself a sheeppig, while Ludo, an anatomical male, considers himself a girlboy. Neither identity claim, sheeppig or girlboy, is completely detached from material "reality"; rather, a trace of materiality comes to bear on the present self-definition. A comparable point might extend to the male lesbian, since the male lesbian does not deny his maleness even as he expands his bodily possibilities into typically excluded regions. The significant issue within this project concerns how these identities are anchored. That is, I have claimed that one is not free to select an identity at will; instead, there must be a basis for an identity. At the same time, I have suggested that what constitutes this "basis" is open to reinterpretation and can be pressed beyond traditional suppositions. On a sexual difference framework, we retain contexts that render certain identities to be either "justified" or not viable. We also admit identities that have even been deemed oxymorons (such as "male lesbian" or "lesbian mother").

Thus, sexual difference theories, and the ways that they can be advanced, can serve to inform broader efforts at reconfiguring identities. If oppression "robs people of their identities," as Birt (1998) suggests, then self-naming and self-definition are powerful means by which to counter oppressive systems. However, to emphasize "self-identity" does not imply that all identities are capable of adoption by all individuals. The case of the white African American discussed earlier, I have maintained, is still problematic since such an identity does not adequately account for material reality and context. The "whiteness" of the so-called white African American's body is positioned within systems of power and privilege that do not interpret (or render) "white" and "black" bodies in the same way. This difference in significance demonstrates that the relationship between bodies and identities is mitigated by context (including social structures) and by cultural realities that interact in considering those identities.

Consequently, bodies as lived are positioned in an in-between region that underscores the fact that bodies "matter" to the meanings that emerge from the adoption or refusal of certain (gendered, raced, sexed) characteristics. In-between bodies offer sites of theoretical investigation, while their very existence acts to unhinge particular theoretical constructs. As a result, the relationship between theory and praxis must be considered as mutually supporting, with theory addressing praxis and praxis anchoring theory. As with the rethinking of bodies themselves, the praxis-theory relation would be neither one of divisive difference nor of merged sameness. Rather, this relation, like the others discussed here, would be a matter of uncovering a new (third) possibility. Such "new" relations likewise emerge from considering what transpires in-between traditional bodily constructs. Rather than marking spaces of invisibility, such regions become sites of reconfigured possibilities.

NOTES

CHAPTER ONE. EMBODIMENT, CONTINGENCY, AND AMBIGUITY

1. Other feminists who make the point that Western dualism subordinates women to men include: Edwards (1989; see below), Gatens (1991), Grosz (1994), Lloyd (1989), Spelman (1988), and Tuana (1990).

2. For a discussion of Beauvoir, see chapter 6 of Lloyd (1984), and chapter 2 of Chanter (1995).

3. Anne Edwards also makes this point nicely in her article, "The Sex/Gender Distinction: Has It Outlived Its Usefulness?" (1989). Edwards states: "The important question of how best to represent relationships between complex, diverse, and mutually interdependent phenomena has been preempted by the imposition of a preferred model, that of an either/or dichotomous division, with its attendant emphasis on difference and opposition rather than similarity and overlap, and a privileging of one of the alternatives in each binary pair" (1989, 7). For Irigaray, however, the issue is of thinking "difference" in a way other than in terms of mutual exclusion—a difference that, Irigaray argues, has never been thought.

4. I am placing "sexual" within parentheses, here and elsewhere, to emphasize the fact that *sexual* difference has always been conceived on a hierarchical basis; but that *difference*, as a broader question, has been subjected to the same hierarchy.

5. In an updated preface to *In A Different Voice*, Carol Gilligan states, "It seems obvious to me, as a psychologist, that differences in the body . . . would make a difference psychologically" (1993, xi). If followed through, this remark by Gilligan would connect my present focus on embodiment and sexual difference with the issue of ethics, since Gilligan refers to "responsibility ethics" as the "psychologic logic of relationships" rather than the "formal logic of fairness" (which informs the justice approach). An ethics of care is contextual in its emphasis on seeing connections (Gilligan 1993, 45). This emphasis stands in contrast to "[t]he voice that set the dominant key in ethics, which was keyed to separation," according to Gilligan, "the separate self, the individual acting alone" (1995, 121). Thus, comparable to Irigaray's project, Gilligan's research has involved a (re)thinking of relationships—or the *relation between*—and revealing a masculine bias.

6. Grosz points out that "the sexual specificity of the body and the ways sexual difference produces or effects truth, knowledge, justice, etc. has never been thought. The role of the specific male body as the body productive of a certain kind of knowledge (objective, verifiable, causal, quantifiable) has never been theorized" (1994, 4). Referring to the unique role played by Descartes in the "masculinization" of knowledge, Grosz states, "Descartes succeeded in linking the mind-body opposition

to the foundations of knowledge itself, a link which places the mind in a position of hierarchical superiority over and above nature, including the nature of the body" (6).

7. On the one-sex model, according to Laqueur, women's bodies were biologically or medically conceived to be fundamentally the same as men's (for example, women were considered "inverted men"). On the two-sex model, women's bodies are depicted as inherently different from men's (that is, women are rendered as "opposed" to men).

8. As Grosz indicates, theorists of sexual difference differ from social constructionists—as well as from egalitarian feminists—in that social constructionists also retain a mind/body dualism. On a social constructionist view, Grosz states, "[T]he mind is regarded as a social, cultural, and historical object; bodies provide the base, the raw materials for the inculcation of interpellation into ideology. . . . Political struggles are thus directed toward neutralization of the sexually specific body" (1994, 17).

9. Gatens cites Lloyd (1984), Grimshaw (1986), and Gatens (1991).

10. See, for example, Butler (1986, 44).

CHAPTER TWO. IRIGARAY'S (RE)FIGURING OF SPACE-TIME AND PLACE

1. Women have been thought to achieve equality with men when biology is detached from convention, when sex is split from gender. On the other hand, women have been rendered subordinate to men when biology dictates their role/function, when sex *requires* their gender. To the extent that women have been linked with a presumed biological function, their sex seems to demand their gender. Women, as a sex, have been characterized to engender roles of "household provider," "instrument," "passive receptacle," etc.

2. Elizabeth Spelman and Julia Annas raise significant objections to "standard" feminist, scholarly literature on Aristotle and Plato. Spelman argues that feminists "have not been attentive to the fact that when Aristotle talks about 'woman's nature' or 'man's nature' he isn't talking about all women . . ." or men (1988, 47). Rather, Spelman indicates, when Aristotle "speaks of the differences between 'men and women,' he is distinguishing between men and women of a particular class, the citizen class" (46). On Aristotle's account, Spelman points out, "One can't tell from the fact that there is a female body whether one is in the presence of a 'woman' or a female slave" (44). The status of female slaves has either been ignored, or considered "of no real significance for the understanding of the place of 'women,'" Spelman claims (47). Concerning Plato, Annas argues against representations of Plato as "the first feminist" (1979, 24)—contending that Plato's proposals with respect to women "are justified entirely by the resulting benefit to the state and not at all by women's needs or rights" (31). Plato's argument for women's equality in the ideal city "is not based on, and makes no reference to, women's desires and needs" (Annas 1979, 28). In opposition to modern liberal arguments that maintain that "women should have equal opportunities with men because otherwise they lead stunted and unhappy lives" (29), Annas indicates it is merely women's "usefulness to the state" that grounds Plato's reasoning.

3. Irigaray states, "All those who advocate equality need to come to terms with the fact that their claims produce a greater and greater split between the so-called equal units and those authorities . . . used to measure or out-measure them"

(1993b, vi). As men have defined women in relation to men (that is, to themselves), in seeking inclusion within a masculine standard, feminists have maintained this same measure. Wanting to be equal *to* men, women remain defined only in relation to a masculine subject.

4. In a footnote to a discussion of Irigaray's reading of Plato's *Timaeus*, Butler states, "For a discussion of a notion of an 'interval' which is neither exclusively space nor time, see Irigaray's reading of Aristotle's Physics, 'Le Lieu, l'intervalle,' *Ethique de la différence sexuelle*, pp. 41–62" (1993a, 252 n 16). I am suggesting that such a notion of the interval is already addressed by Irigaray in her reading of Diotima's discourse in the *Symposium* and that such discussion is not delayed until Irigaray's subsequent essay on Aristotle.

5. All references to the *Symposium* are noted in the text and correspond to the standard paragraph number. I have used Walter Hamilton's translation (Plato 1971).

6. Regarding a notion of the interval (the "in-between") that Diotima represents, and its relation to Aristophanes' conception of love, Irigaray states, "This threshold appears to be blocked, notably in the myth of Aristophanes in the *Symposium*, if I need to give an example" (1993b, 46). Whereas an unbridgeable gap arises when the original creature is split in half, the gap is replaced with a fusion when the two halves are reunited in love. "In love," Irigaray suggests, "it would be fitting if the parts of the whole—the union of man and woman—enveloped one another *mutually* and not destroy one another's envelopes" (46). Such a (re)conception of love is offered in the first part of Diotima's discourse, I suggest, pointing to a relation between men and women of the sort that interests Irigaray.

7. Alexander Nehamas and Paul Woodruff make this suggestion in the Introduction to their translation of the *Symposium* (1989, xii–xiii). Nehamas and Woodruff go on to claim that the reference to Aristophanes' speech also indicates that the second part of Diotima's speech is likely to represent the view of Plato (xiii).

8. Andrea Nye cites Nussbaum as one commentator, among many, who not only adheres to the fictional status of Diotima, but who simply assumes it (1992, 90 n 1). There are, however, good reasons for regarding Diotima (that is, the Diotima of the *Symposium*) as a fictional device of Plato—reasons independent of whether there existed an actual historical personage by that name. Nye criticizes Irigaray's reading as "ahistorical." However, the "Diotima" that Irigaray considers is neither historical nor ahistorical; rather, she is rightly "placed" within a dialogue of Plato.

9. See also, Chanter (1995, 301 n 60).

10. Nye seems to overlook the importance of "miscarries" (*échoue*) in attributing to Irigaray the more mundane claim that Diotima's method "fails" (1992, 79). However, "fails" has the sense of "to lose strength," "to weaken," "to fade or die away," "to stop functioning," "to fall short," "to be deficient in." "Fails," that is, is more passive than "miscarries" in that for a method to fail is for it simply not to succeed. Irigaray, on the contrary, seems to intend the stronger claim.

11. For a discussion of the occurrence, and significance, of midwife and birthing imagery in the *Symposium*, see Burnyeat, who indicates "the sustained use [Plato] makes of the imagery [of the midwife] . . . in the *Symposium*, where the idea of mental pregnancy and birth is central to Diotima's discourse on love . . ." (1992, 54).

12. Compare to Chanter: "That Diotima is said to miscarry could be due to Diotima's inability to bring to fruition the thought that, on Irigaray's account, she had begun to bear. Or again, it could be due to the incompetence of the midwife,

Socrates" (1995, 161). I have only attempted to follow through the second sort of interpretation.

13. Compare to Whitford: "Female sexuality has always been conceptualized on the basis of masculine parameters" (1991, 150; Irigaray 1985b, 23). Whitford states, "the orgasm, a kind of technical criterion of 'success,' [has] more to do with the requirements of male sexuality than with a possible different sexuality" (Whitford 1991, 150; Irigaray 1985b, 23).

14. Irigaray states, "We must reexamine our history thoroughly to understand why this sexual difference has not had its chance to develop. . . . It is surely a question of the dissociation of body and soul, of sexuality and spirituality, of the lack of a passage . . . between the inside and the outside, the outside and the inside" (1993a, 114–15). An interesting connection, here, is Grosz's *Volatile Bodies* (1994), which is divided into two main sections: "The Inside Out" and "The Outside In." Grosz undermines dualistic views of the subject by discussing both how the subject's "psychical interior" acts to form a body as a *specific type* of exteriority (from the inside out), and how "social inscriptions" on the body's surface serve to produce a psychical interiority (from the outside in). Grosz examines the relation between mind (or psyche) and body—revealing them, not as two distinct entities, but as integrally bound up with one another.

15. As Diprose states, "What must be examined in an ethics of sexual difference, according to Irigaray, is the 'economy of the interval' between the (male) subject and discourse, between the subject and his world and between the subject and woman" (1994, 36).

16. "Apollo," Aristophanes explains, "tied the skin tightly in the middle of the bellly round a single aperture which men call the navel" (191C).

17. As Jacqueline Rose indicates, regarding Lacanian psychoanalysis, "The duality of the relation between mother and child must be broken. . . . In Lacan's account, the phallus stands for that moment of rupture. It refers mother and child to the dimension of the symbolic which is figured by the father's place. The mother is taken to desire the phallus not because she contains it . . . but because she does not" (1983, Introduction II, 38).

18. All references to Aristotle's Physics IV, 1–5 are cited in the text by line number and are to *The Complete Works of Aristotle: The Revised Oxford Translation*, ed. Johnathan Barnes, trans. R. P. Hardie and R. K. Gaye. Princeton: Princeton University Press, 1984.

19. Chanter connects Irigaray's reading of Aristotle on place with Heidegger's reading of Aristotle on time. Chanter also demonstrates a parallel between Irigaray's concern with sexual difference and Heidegger's focus on Being. See especially chapter 4, *Ethics of Eros: Irigaray's Rewriting of the Philosophers*. Also with respect to Heidegger, the essay "The Thing" (1971)—in which Heidegger speaks of the void and the vessel—is in the background to the discussion of "void" and "vessel" in the present chapter.

20. Of Aristotle's definition of place, Irigaray states:

> The boundary of the "containing body" can be understood of the womb. . . .
> But sexual desire that goes toward the womb and no longer returns to it also
> goes toward infinity since it never touches the boundary of the "containing
> body." Instead of perceiving the body that contains it *hic et nunc*, it goes
> toward another container. . . . So there is never any idea that the boundary

of the containing body might be the skin . . . the boundary of the containing body might be the bodily identity of woman. (1993a, 50)

21. Compare to Heidegger: "The thingness of the thing remains concealed,
forgotten" (1971, 170). The "thingness resides in its being *qua* vessel" (169).

22. It is interesting to note that the question that men sometimes ask their
pregnant wives/partners is: "Can we have sex?," or "Will I hurt the baby?" To keep
with Irigaray, it seems that this question arises not so much from medical fact or
concern as from a certain conception of place (vis-à-vis women). That is, the question occurs due to the conceptual collapse of women's sexual and reproductive "function" into one place.

23. It can be said that the association of "woman" with the material cause and
"man" with the efficient cause—thereby rendering women as inferior to men a priori—
builds women's exclusion into the very structure of reality.

24. See Irigaray's essays on Freud and Hegel, "The Blind Spot of an Old
Dream of Symmetry" and "The Eternal Irony of the Community," in *Speculum of the
Other Woman*.

25. Compare to the following remark by Irigaray:

The relation of the little boy to his mother is different from the little girl's
relation. The little boy, in order to situate himself vis-à-vis the mother,
must have a strategy, perhaps a strategy of mastery, because he finds himself
in an extremely difficult situation. He's a little boy. He has come out of a
woman who's different from him. . . . He is therefore in a space of unfath-
omable mystery. He must invent a strategy to keep himself from being
submerged, engulfed. For the little girl it's entirely different. She's a little
woman born of another woman. She is able to engender like her mother,
she has a sort of jubilation in being herself and playing with herself. For the
little boy, it's necessary to construct a world in order to construct himself.
(Irigaray 1995, 107–108)

26. Indeed, "woman" *cannot* exist except insofar as she contains men/children.
On Aristotle's account, matter has no sort of independent existence (thus, neither
does "woman" insofar as she is associated with, and relegated to, matter/the material).
Compare to Hussey: "Aristotle's criticism of Plato is that there is in fact (that is,
within the Aristotelian system) no kind of matter which can persist independently
of the body it serves as the matter of" (1983, xxxii).

CHAPTER THREE. CONTINGENCY AND RACE

1. Gilman is quoting J. J. Virey.

2. For a brief discussion of Gilman's article, see hooks 1992, 62–63.

3. Davis (1993) describes five key beliefs that comprise racist ideology. The
belief that "race causes culture" is one of these.

4. That is, insofar as "culture" informs a "mindset" or "way of thinking." As
Davis explains, the racist belief here is "that race causes culture, that each inbred
population has a distinct culture that is generally transmitted along with its physical
traits" (1993, 24).

5. See, for example, Eduardo Bonilla-Silva's, *White Supremacy and Racism in the Post-Civil Rights Era* (2001).

6. See Davis who describes the negative reaction in the black community to "acting white" (1993, 138).

7. Recall chapter 1, where Gatens is quoted, "It is not masculinity *per se* that is valorized in our culture but the masculine male" (1991, 151).

8. Hooks suggests that "[t]o love blackness is dangerous in a white supremacist culture—so threatening, so serious a breach in the fabric of the social order, that death is the punishment" (1992, 9). The "fact" of Clare's blackness—or knowledge that under a "white" exterior lies "blackness"—leads to Clare's death.

9. As Davis points out, the notion of "one-drop" has had various interpretations (1993, 5).

10. However, "black" cannot simply, or entirely, assume "white" positioning or vice versa. There will always be a "residue" or "remainder"—to use terms from Butler and Irigaray (cf. Butler 1993, 163; Irigaray 1993, 14)—something not contained, or able to cohere, within the attempted substitution. Knowledge of this residue is arguably held by the person attempting to pass (as white), but who fears being "found out."

CHAPTER FOUR. TRANGENDER BODIES

1. Feinberg writes:

> All together, our many communities challenge *all* sex and gender borders and restrictions. The glue that cements these diverse communities together is the defense of the right of each individual to define themselves. As I write this book, the word *trans* is being used increasingly by the gender community as a term uniting the entire coalition. If the term had already enjoyed popular recognition, I would have titled the book *Trans Warriors*. But since the word *transgender* is still most recognizable to people all over the world, I use it in its most inclusive sense: to refer to all those courageous trans warriors of every sex and gender—those who led battles and rebellions throughout history and those who today muster the courage to battle for their identities and for their very lives. (1996, xi)

2. Trans-bodies are not, of course, the only bodies so situated. In terms of the sex/gender distinction, however, trans-bodies maintain a rather unique "position."

3. Public restrooms are exemplary and notorious sites of trans/gender phobia. As Scholinski remarks:

> When I was in a bar in Santa Monica recently, I stood in line for the women's bathroom. The woman ahead of me turned and said, as if to enlighten an idiot, *This is the line for the women's room*. I've heard this statement a lot. I said, "I know." I looked at her as if she was the fool but inside I was sweating. She reminded me again. I said, "I am a woman." I hated saying that; I have never quite fit in that box. She said, "You don't look like a woman. You don't sound like a woman." What was I supposed to do with that? I was like, "What, do you want to see my i.d.?" I pulled

my i.d. out of my wallet; I knew I didn't have to do this but I figured it would end the situation. She took my i.d. and passed it up the line. Each woman looked at my i.d., looked at me, looked at my i.d., looked at each other. (1997, 194)

And, as Feinberg comments:

Now, what happens when butches walk into the women's bathroom? Women nudge each other with elbows, or roll their eyes, and say mockingly, "Do you know which bathroom you're in?" That's not how women behave when they really believe there's a man in the bathroom. This scenario is not about women's safety—it's an example of gender-phobia. And ask yourself, if you were in a women's bathroom, and there were two teenage drag queens putting on lipstick in front of the mirror, would you be in danger? If you called security or the cops, or forced those drag queens to use the men's room, would they be safe? (1996, 117)

4. Feinberg conveys:

Brandon Teena, a young white man, moved to a small town in Nebraska in 1993. After a minor brush with the law, the police reportedly exposed the fact that Brandon had been born female. A short time later, Brandon was forcibly stripped at a Christmas party in front of a woman he had dated, and then was kidnapped, beaten, and gang-raped. Yet police refused to pursue charges against the two men Brandon named as his attackers. On New Year's Day, Brandon and two other people were found shot to death; Brandon's body was repeatedly stabbed. (1996, 132)

5. The four main components of the diagnostic criteria for Gender Identity Disorder are:

"A. A strong and persistent cross-gender identification (not merely a desire for any perceived cultural advantages of being the other sex) . . . B. Persistent discomfort with his or her sex or sense of inappropriateness in the gender role of that sex . . . C. The disturbance causes clinically significant distress or impairment in social, occupational, or other important areas of functioning" (cited in Scholinski 1997, 205–206, from the Diagnostic and Statistical Manual of Mental Disorders, Fourth Edition. Washington, DC: American Psychiatric Association, 1994).

6. Scholinski is ordered to overcome her boyish behaviors and appearance at a cost, she notes, of one million dollars in paid health benefits.
7. A great discussion of this concern can be seen in an article by Lillian Faderman in The Advocate, entitled, "Why is it shocking when a lesbian leader falls for a man" (April 29, 1997). Faderman states:

Shock waves pass through some enclaves of the lesbian community every time it happens [when lesbian leaders fall for men]. . . . Observation tells us that the neat categories of sexual identity are often an illusion. . . . The narrow categories of identity politics are obviously deceptive. They hide the complex, multifaceted nature of human beings. . . . That being so, how can we not feel discomfort or loss or annoyance when anything or anyone reminds us how simplistic and unstable the notion of identity truly is. (80)

8. For example, Halberstam indicates:

[F]ar from being an imitation of maleness, female masculinity actually affords us a glimpse of how masculinity is constructed as masculinity. In other words, female masculinities are framed as the rejected scraps of dominant masculinity in order that male masculinity may appear to be the real thing. . . . But what we understand as heroic masculinity has been produced by and across both male and female bodies. (1998, 1–2)

CHAPTER FIVE. COMPETING NARRATIVES IN LGBTQ STUDIES

The paper on which this chapter is based was co-authored with Kendal L. Broad, University of Florida. I have used the first person throughout this chapter in order to maintain a consistent voice throughout the book; however, the ideas in this chapter are shared and should be recognized as such. For additional discussion of some of the issues raised in this chapter, see also Broad and Bloodsworth (2001).

1. In keeping with the logic of identity, I refer to gay/lesbian/bisexual/transgender identity politics and pedagogies in identity terms—LGBT. I use "queer" to signify a discussion of queer (identity blurring [Gamson 1998]) politics and pedagogies. When discussing the interplay between identity and anti-identity, I refer to both with the abbreviation LGBTQ.

2. In this chapter, in relation to queer theory/queer pedagogy, I use the term *anti-identity* to refer to the sort of deconstruction of identity categories that this theory/pedagogy tends to promote; that is, the disruption of traditional, static notions of identity in favor of fluid renderings of them. Thus, the term *queer* counters traditional notions (and this countering includes construing the term positively in light of a negative history). I do not use "anti-identity" to suggest a wholesale rejection of "identity" on the part of queer theory/queer pedagogy nor to imply that queer theory/queer pedagogy sees "identity" as an outright mistake.

3. While I focus on the lesbian and gay studies classroom here, I would argue that many points raised in this chapter could be applied to other classes as well—especially those framed by "identities" and "subjectivities"—both individual and communal.

4. Notably, there are increasing efforts to theorize feminist poststructural and postmodern pedagogies. However, in this piece, I focus on feminist standpoint pedagogies because they have figured as central.

5. Only recently has "transgender" been included in LGBT groups in the United States and, as yet, little has been written about transgender pedagogy per se. The one exception is recent work by the Intersex Society of North American about how to teach intersexuality in a feminist classroom (Koyama and Chase 2001).

Importantly, given the interplay between identity and anti-identity in transgender social movement action (Broad 2003), it is likely that work creating a sort of "transgender" pedagogy would reflect both identity and anti-identity strategies.

6. These examples are from student in-class assignments in Mary's and Kendal's classes during the summer and fall semesters of 2000, and the summer session of 2001.

7. These student comments are from the same classes and assignments as above (note 6).

8. The erasure of identity may be seen as an extreme form of the "anti-identity" project. In this sense, comments that advocate a complete annihilation of identity categories are more extreme than queer theory's/queer pedagogy's relationship to identities (which promote a troubling—but not necessarily a forgetting—of them). See note 2 above.

9. This reference is to Butler (1993) who has played on two senses of "matter"; that is, the materiality (the matter) of bodies and the significance that bodies hold (how bodies matter).

CHAPTER SIX. THE TROUBLE WITH "QUEER"

A version of this chapter entitled, "Sexual Difference Theories and Same-Sex Couples: Is Sexual Difference Theory Heterosexist?," was first presented at the Pacific American Philosophical Association (APA) Meeting in Seattle, Washington, 2002, for the Society for Lesbian and Gay Philosophy (SLGP) and the LGBT Committee on the Status of Lesbian, Gay, Bisexual, and Transgender People in the Profession. Thanks to audience members for helpful comments that led to some revisions of this chapter.

1. Both transgender and transsexual—"transgender" being the umbrella term and "transsexual" referring to either pre- or post-operative persons.

2. For a full discussion of this issue, see C. Richard King, Carmen R. Lugo-Lugo, and Mary K. Bloodsworth-Lugo. Forthcoming. *Animating Difference: Race, Gender, and Sexuality in Contemporary Films for Children*. Lanham, MD: Rowman and Littlefield.

3. Carmen Lugo-Lugo's paper, " 'So You are a Mestiza': Exploring the Consequences of Ethnic and Racial Clumping for Latinas in the U.S. Academy" (forthcoming, *Racial and Ethnic Studies*) was very helpful for my consideration of difficulties with the "LGBTAQQI" alphabet soup phenomenon in this chapter.

REFERENCES

Abelove, Henry, Michele Aina Barale, and David M. Halperin. 1993. *The lesbian and gay studies reader.* New York: Routledge.

Annas, Julia. 1979. Plato's *Republic* and feminism. In *Woman in western thought,* edited by Martha Lee Osborne. New York: Random House.

Appiah, Anthony. 1985. The uncompleted argument: Du Bois and the illusion of race. In *"Race," writing, and difference,* edited by Henry Louis Gates Jr. Chicago: University of Chicago Press.

Aristotle. 1984. Physics IV, 1–5. Translated by R. P. Hardie and R. K. Gaye. In *The complete works of Aristotle: The revised Oxford translation,* edited by Johnathan Barnes. Oxford: Oxford University Press. I: 354–62.

Bakare-Yusuf, Bibi. 1999. The economy of violence: Black bodies and the unspeakable terror. In *Feminist theory and the body,* edited by Janet Price and Margrit Shildrick. New York: Routledge.

Berg, Allison, Jean Kowaleski, Caroline Le Guin, Ellen Weinauer, and Eric A. Wolfe. 1998. Breaking the silence: Sexual preference in the composition classroom. In *The feminist teacher anthology,* edited by Gail E. Cohee, Elisabeth Daumer, Theresa D. Kemp, Paula M. Krebs, Sue A. Lafky, and Sandra Runzo. New York: Teachers College Press.

Bigwood, Carol. 1991. Renaturalizing the body (with a little help from Merleau-Ponty). *Hypatia* 6, no. 3: 54–73.

Birt, Robert. 1998. Existence, identity, and liberation. In *Race, class, gender, and sexuality: The big questions,* edited by Naomi Zack, Laurie Shrage, and Crispin Sartwell. Malden, MA: Blackwell.

Bolin, Anne. 1988. *In search of Eve: Transsexual rites of passage.* New York: Bergin and Garvey.

Bonilla-Silva, Eduardo. 2001. *White supremacy and racism in the post–civil rights era.* Boulder: Lynne Rienner.

Bordo, Susan. 1987. *The flight to objectivity: Essays on Cartesianism and culture.* Albany: State University of New York Press.

Bornstein, Kate. 1994. *Gender outlaw: On men, women, and the rest of us.* New York: Routledge.

———. 1997. *My gender workbook: How to become a real man, a real woman, the real you, or something else entirely.* New York: Routledge.

Braidotti, Rosi. 1994. *Nomadic subjects: Embodiment and sexual difference in contemporary feminist theory.* New York: Columbia University Press.

Broad, Kendal L., and Mary K. Bloodsworth. 2001. FemiQueer pedagogies: "Lesbian/gay" studies in postmodern women's studies. *Feminist Teacher* 13, no. 2: 108–24.

Broad, K. L. 2003. Is it G, L, B, *and* T? Gender/sexuality movements and transgender collective identity (de)constructions. *International Journal of Sexuality and Gender Studies* 7, no. 4.

Burnyeat, Myles. 1992. Socratic midwifery, Platonic inspiration. In *Essays on the philosophy of Socrates*, edited by Hugh H. Benson. New York: Oxford University Press. Originally published in *Bulletin of the Institute of Classical Studies* 24 (1977): 7–16.

Butler, Judith. 1986. Sex and gender in Simone de Beauvoir's *Second Sex*. *Yale French Studies* 72: 35–49.

———. 1990. *Gender trouble: Feminism and the subversion of identity*. New York: Routledge.

———. 1993. *Bodies that matter: On the discursive limits of "sex."* New York: Routledge.

———. 1997. Against proper objects. In *Feminism meets queer theory*, edited by Elizabeth Weed and Naomi Schor. Bloomington: Indiana University Press, 1–30.

Caldwell, Anne. 2002. Transforming sacrifice: Irigaray and the politics of sexual difference. *Hypatia* 17, no. 4: 16–38.

Califia, Patrick. 2003. *Sex changes: The politics of transgenderism*. San Francisco: Cleis Press.

Cameron, Loren. 1996. *Body alchemy: Transsexual portraits*. San Francisco: Cleis Press.

Chanter, Tina. 1995. *Ethics of Eros: Irigaray's rewriting of the philosophers*. New York: Routledge.

———. Forthcoming. Irigaray's challenge to the fetishistic hegemony of the Platonic one and many. In *Re-writing difference: Luce Irigaray and "the Greeks,"* edited by Elena Varikas and Athena Athanasion. Albany: State University of New York Press.

Chesler, Mark A. 1991. Dealing with prejudice and conflict in the classroom: The pink triangle exercise. *Teaching Sociology* 19, no. 2: 173–81.

Cohee, Gail E., et al. 1998. *The feminist teacher anthology*. New York: Teachers College Press.

Cromwell, Jason. 1999. *Transmen and ftms: Identities, bodies, genders, and sexualities*. Champaign: University of Illinois Press.

Davis, James. 1993. *Who is black? One nation's definition*. Philadelphia: The University of Pennsylvania Press.

Davis, Kathy. 1997. *Embodied practices: Feminist perspectives on the body*. Thousand Oaks, CA: Sage.

Diprose, Rosalyn. 1994. *The bodies of women: Ethics, embodiment, and sexual difference*. New York: Routledge.

Du Cille, Anne. 1996. The occult of true black womanhood: Critical demeanor and black feminist studies. In *The second signs reader*, edited by Ruth-Ellen B. Joeres and Barbara Laslett. Chicago: The University of Chicago Press.

Edwards, Anne. 1989. The sex/gender distinction: Has it outlived its usefulness? *Australian Feminist Studies* 10 (Summer): 1–12.

Eng, David L., and Alice Y. Hom, editors. 1998. *Q&A: Queer in Asian America*. Philadelphia: Temple University Press.

Faderman, Lillian. 1997. Why is it shocking when a lesbian leader falls for a man? *The Advocate*, April 29.

Feinberg, Leslie. 1996. *Transgender warriors: Making history from Joan of Arc to Dennis Rodman*. Boston: Beacon Press.

Fox Keller, Evelyn. 1985. *Reflections on gender and science*. New Haven: Yale University Press.

Freeman, Barbara. 1988. (Re)writing patriarchal texts: The *Symposium*. In *Postmodernism and continental philosophy*, edited by Silverman. Albany: State University of New York Press.

Fuss, Diana. 1989. *Essentially speaking: Feminism, nature, and difference*. New York: Routledge.

Gamson, Joshua. 1998. Must identity movements self-destruct? A queer dilemma. In *Social perspectives in lesbian and gay studies: A reader*, edited by Peter M. Nardi and Beth E. Schneider. New York: Routledge. Originally published in *Social Problems* 42, no. 3 (1995): 390–407.

Gatens, Moira. 1991. A critique of the sex/gender distinction. In *A reader in feminist knowledge*, edited by Sneja Gunew. London: Routledge. Originally published in *Beyond Marxism? Interventions after Marx*, edited by J. Allen and P. Patton. NSW: Intervention Publications, 1983. Also chapter 1 of *Imaginary bodies*.

———. 1996. *Imaginary bodies: Ethics, power, and corporeality*. New York: Routledge.

Gilligan, Carol. 1993. *In a different voice: Psychological theory and women's development*. Cambridge: Harvard University Press.

———. 1995. Hearing the difference: Theorizing connection. *Hypatia* 10, no. 2 (Spring): 120–27.

Gilman, Sander L. 1985. Black bodies, white bodies: Toward an iconography of female sexuality in late nineteenth-century art, medicine, and literature. In *"Race," writing, and difference*, edited by Henry Louis Gates Jr. Chicago: The University of Chicago Press.

Gordon, Lewis. 1997. Race, sex, and matrices of desire in an antiblack world. In *Race/sex: Their sameness, difference, and interplay*, edited by Naomi Zack. New York: Routledge.

Grimshaw, J. 1986. *Feminist philosophers: Women's perspectives on philosophical traditions*. Brighton: Harvester.

Grosz, Elizabeth. 1994. *Volatile bodies: Toward a corporeal feminism*. Bloomington and Indianapolis: Indiana University Press.

Halberstam, Judith. 1998. *Female masculinity*. Durham: Duke University Press.

Hammonds, Evelynn. 1994. Black (w)holes and the geometry of black female sexuality. *differences* 6, no. 2–3. Bloomington: Indiana University Press.

———. 1999. Toward a genealogy of black female sexuality: The problematic of silence. In *Feminist theory and the body*, edited by Janet Price and Margrit Shildrick. New York: Routledge.

Harding, Sandra. 1987. *Feminism & methodology*. Bloomington: Indiana University Press.

Hass, Marjorie. 2000. The style of the speaking subject: Irigaray's empirical studies of language production. *Hypatia* 15, no. 10: 64–89.

Heidegger, Martin. 1971. The thing. In *Poetry, language, thought*, translated by Albert Hofstadter. New York: Harper and Row.

Holloway, Karla. 1987. African values and western chaos. In *New dimensions of spirituality: A biracial and bicultural reading of the novels of Toni Morrison*, edited by Karla Holloway and Stephanie A. Demetrakopoulos. New York: Greenwood Press.

hooks, bell. 1992. *Black looks: Race and representation*. Boston: South End Press.

———. 1994. *Teaching to transgress: Education as the practice of freedom*. New York: Routledge.

Hughes, Langston. 1986. Cross. In *The life of Langston Hughes*, Vol. 1. By Arnold
      Rampersand. New York: Oxford University Press.

Huntington, Patricia. 1997. Fragmentation, race, and gender: Building solidarity in
      the postmodern era. In *Existence in black: An anthology of black existential
      philosophy*, edited by Lewis R. Gordon. New York: Routledge.

Hussey, Edward. 1983. *Aristotle's Physics Books III and IV, translated with notes*. New
      York: Oxford University Press.

Irigaray, Luce. 1985a. *Speculum of the other woman*. Translated by Gillian C. Gill.
      New York: Cornell University Press.

———. 1985b. *This sex which is not one*. Translated by Catherine Porter and Carolyn
      Burke. Ithaca: Cornell University Press.

———. 1991. Questions to Emmanuel Levinas. In *The Irigaray reader*. Translated and
      edited by Margaret Whitford. Oxford: Blackwell. Also in *Re-reading Levinas*,
      edited by Robert Bernasconi and Simon Critchley. Bloomington and India-
      napolis: Indiana University Press, 1991.

———. 1992. Sorcerer love: A reading of Plato's Symposium, Diotima's speech. Trans-
      lated by Eleanor Kuykendall. In *Revaluing French feminism*, edited by Nancy
      Fraser and Sandra Lee Bartky. Bloomington and Indianapolis: Indiana Univer-
      sity Press. Originally published in *Hypatia* 3, no. 3 (Winter 1989): 32–44.

———. 1993a. *An ethics of sexual difference*. Translated by Carolyn Burke and Gillian
      C. Gill. New York: Cornell University Press. *Ethique de la difference sexuelle*.
      Paris: Minuit, 1984.

———. 1993b. Belief itself. In *Sexes and genealogies*, translated by Gillian C. Gill.
      New York: Columbia University Press.

———. 1995. "Je—Luce Irigaray": A meeting with Luce Irigaray. Interview with
      Elizabeth Hirsh and Gary A. Olson. Translated by Elizabeth Hirsh and Gaeton
      Brulette. *Hypatia* 10, no. 2 (Spring 1995): 93–114.

———. 1996. *I love to you*. Translated by Alison Martin. New York: Routledge.

Jaggar, Alison. 1990. Sexual difference and sexual equality. In *Theoretical perspectives on
      sexual difference*, edited by Deborah L. Rhode. New Haven: Yale University Press.

Jagose, Annamarie. 1997. *Queer theory: An introduction*. New York: New York Uni-
      versity Press.

King, C. Richard, Carmen R. Lugo-Lugo, and Mary K. Bloodsworth-Lugo. Forthcom-
      ing. *Animating difference: Race, gender, and sexuality in contemporary films for
      children*. Lanham, MD: Rowman and Littlefield.

Kivel, Paul. 2002. *Uprooting racism: How white people can work for racial justice*. Gabriola
      Island, Canada: New Society Publishers.

Koyama, Emi (emi@isna.org) and Cheryl Chase (info@isna.org). 2001. Teaching kit
      for women's, gender, and queer studies instructors, *Intersex Society of North
      America*, http://www.isna.org/pr/pr6-11-01.html.

Kuykendall, Eleanor. 1992. Introduction to "Sorcerer Love," by Luce Irigaray. In
      Revaluing French feminism, edited by Nancy Fraser and Sandra Lee Bartky.
      Bloomington and Indianapolis: Indiana University Press. Originally published
      in *Hypatia* 3, no. 3 (Winter 1989): 28–31.

Laqueur, Thomas. 1990. *Making sex: Body and gender from the Greeks to Freud*. Cam-
      bridge: Harvard University Press.

Larsen, Nella. 1994. *Quicksand and passing*. Edited by Deborah E. McDowell. New
      Brunswick: Rutgers University Press.

Lear, Johnathan. 1988. *Aristotle: The desire to understand*. New York: Cambridge University Press.

Lloyd, Genevieve. 1984. *The man of reason: "Male" and "female" in Western philosophy*. Minneapolis: University of Minnesota Press.

———. 1989. Woman as other: Sex, gender, and subjectivity. *Australian Feminist Studies* 10 (Summer): 13–22.

Lugo-Lugo, Carmen R. Forthcoming. "So you are a Mestiza": Exploring the consequences of ethnic and racial clumping for Latinas in the U.S. academy. *Racial and Ethnic Studies*.

Lugones, María. 1996. Purity, impurity, and separation. In *The Second Signs reader*, edited by Ruth-Ellen B. Joeres and Barbara Laslett. Chicago: The University of Chicago Press.

———. 1998. El pasar discontinuo de la cachapera/tortillera del barrio a la barra al movimiento (The discontinuous passing of the cachapera/torillera from the barrio to the bar to the movement). In *Daring to be good: Essays in feminist ethico-politics*, edited by Bat-Ami Bar On and Ann Ferguson. New York: Routledge.

Mann, Susan A., and Lori A. Kelley. 1997. Standing at the crossroads of modernist thought: Collins, Smith, and the new feminist epistemologies. *Gender & Society* 11, no. 4: 391–408.

McLaren, Peter. 1997. Paolo Freire's legacy of hope and struggle. *Theory, Culture & Society* 14, no. 4: 147–53.

Messer-Davidow, Ellen. 1989. The philosophical bases of feminist literary criticisms. In *Gender & theory: Dialogues on feminist criticism*, edited by L. Kauffman. Oxford: Basil Blackwell.

Mohanram, Radhika. 1999. *Black body*. Minneapolis: University of Minnesota Press.

Moraga, Cherríe, and Gloria Anzaldúa, editors. 1983. *This bridge called my back: Writings by radical women of color*. New York: Kitchen Table, Women of Color Press.

Morrison, Toni. 1981. *Tar baby*. New York: Plume.

Murara, Luisa. 1994. Female genealogies. In *Engaging with Irigaray: Feminist philosophy and modern European thought*, edited by Carolyn Burke, Naomi Schor, and Margaret Whitford. New York: Columbia University Press.

Nardi, Peter M., and Beth E. Schneider, editors. 1998. *Social perspectives in lesbian and gay studies: A reader*. New York: Routledge.

Nehamas, Alexander, and Paul Woodruff. 1989. *Plato's Symposium*. Indianapolis: Hackett.

Nussbaum, Martha. 1986. *The fragility of goodness: Luck and ethics in Greek tragedy and philosophy*. New York: Cambridge University Press.

Nye, Andrea. 1992. The hidden host: Irigaray and Diotima at Plato's Symposium. In *Revaluing French feminism*, edited by Nancy Fraser and Sandra Lee Bartky. Bloomington and Indianapolis: Indiana University Press. Originally published in *Hypatia* 3, no. 3 (Winter 1989): 45–61.

Okin, Susan Moller. 1979. *Women in Western political thought*. Princeton: Princeton University Press.

Olkowski, Dorothea. 2000. The end of phenomenology: Bergson's interval in Irigaray. *Hypatia* 15, no. 3: 73–91.

Outlaw, Lucius. 1996. *On race and philosophy*. New York: Routledge.

Pellegrini, Ann, and Paul B. Franklin. 1996. Queer collaborations: Feminist pedagogy. In *The new lesbian studies: Into the twenty-first century*. New York: The Feminist Press.

Plato. 1971. *The symposium*. Translated by Walter Hamilton. New York: Viking Penquin.

Plymire, Darcy C. 2000. Teaching gender in lesbian and gay studies. *NWSA Journal* 12, no. 1: 174–80.

Rose, Jacqueline. 1983. Introduction II. In *Feminine sexuality: Jacques Lacan and the ecole freudienne*, edited by Juliet Mitchell and Jacqueline Rose. New York: Pantheon Books.

Rothenberg, Paula. 1998. Incorporating race, class, gender into feminist pedagogy. In *The feminist teacher anthology*, edited by Gail E. Cohee, Elsabeth Daumer, Theresa D. Kemp, Paula M. Krebs, Sue A. Lafky, and Sandra Runzo. New York: Teachers College Press.

Rubin, Gayle. 1975. The traffic in women: Notes on the "political economy" of sex. In *Toward an anthropology of women*, edited by R. R. Reiter. New York: Monthly Review Press.

Scholinski, Daphne. 1997. *The last time I wore a dress*. New York: Riverhead.

Seidman, Steven. 1994. Queer pedagogy/queer-ing sociology. *Critical Sociology* 20, no. 3: 169–76.

Shrage, Laurie. 1997. Passing beyond the other race or sex. In *Race/sex: Their sameness, difference, and interplay*, edited by Naomi Zack. New York: Routledge.

Sjöholm, Cecilia. 2000. Crossing lovers: Luce Irigaray's elemental passions. *Hypatia* 15, no. 30: 92–112.

Smith, Nicholas. 1983. Plato and Aristotle on the nature of women. *Journal of the History of Philosophy* 21, no. 4 (October): 467–78.

Spelman, Elizabeth. 1988. *Inessential woman: Problems of exclusion in feminist thought*. Boston: Beacon Press.

Stone, Sandy. 1991. The "empire" strikes back: A posttranssexual manifesto. In *Body guards: The cultural politics of gender ambiguity*, edited by Kristina Straub and Julia Epstein. New York: Routledge.

Tate, Greg. 2003. *Everything but the burden: What white people are taking from black culture*. New York: Harlem Moon.

Taylor, A. E. 1966. *Plato: The man and his work*. London: Butler and Tanner Ltd.

Tuana, Nancy. 1990. Re-fusing nature/nurture. In *Hypatia reborn*. Bloomington: Indiana University Press.

Valerio, Max Wolf. 2002. "Now that you're a white man": Changing sex in a postmodern world—being, becoming, and borders. In *This bridge we call home: Radical visions for transformation*, edited by Gloria E. Anzaldúa and Analouise Keating. New York: Routledge.

Wallace, Julia. 1994. Queer-ing sociology in the classroom. *Critical Sociology* 20, no. 3: 177–92.

Walters, Suzanna Danuta. 1996. From here to queer: Radical feminism, postmodernism, and the lesbian menace (or why can't a woman be more like a fag?). *Signs* 21, no. 4: 830–69.

Washington, Johnny. 1993. "Black" or "African American": What's in a name? In *American mosaic: Selected readings on America's multicultural heritage*, edited by Young I. Song and Eugene K. Kim. New Jersey: Prentice-Hall.

Weed, Elizabeth. 1997. Introduction. In *Feminism meets queer theory*, edited by Elizabeth Weed and Naomi Schor. Bloomington: Indiana University Press.

Wendell, Susan. 1996. *The rejected body: Feminist philosophical reflections on disability*. New York: Routledge.

Whitford, Margaret. 1991. *Luce Irigaray: Philosophy in the feminine*. New York: Routledge.

Wright, Janet. 1998. Lesbian instructor comes out. In *The feminist teacher anthology*, edited by Gail E. Cohee, Elsabeth Daumer, Theresa D. Kemp, Paula M. Krebs, Sue A. Lafky, and Sandra Runzo. New York: Teachers College Press.

Zimmerman, Bonnie. 1996. Placing lesbians. In *The new lesbian studies: Into the twenty-first century*. New York: The Feminist Press.

Zita, Jacquelyn. 1998. *Body talk: Philosophical reflections on sex and gender*. New York: Columbia University Press.

INDEX

"acting white," 50n6, 52
Addams, Calpernia Sarah, 86
Advocate, The, 68n7, 86
African American (term), 50, 79, 91, 98
Alexie, Sherman, 90
ambiguity/ambiguous, 1, 6–8, 21, 31, 39, 42, 64, 75
    both . . . and logic, 66
    love and, 31
    navel as, 43. *See also* navel
androgyny/androgynous, 28–29, 43. *See also* symmetrical relations
    third-sexed creature, 28–30
An Ethics of Sexual Difference (Irigaray), 25, 35
Annas, Julia, 26n2
Antigone, 22–23, 37
anti-identity, 6, 69–70, 69n2, 72n5, 74–81, 79n8, 83
Anzaldúa, Gloria, 79, 95
Apollo, 29, 36n16
Appiah, Anthony, 48
Araujo, Eddie (Gwen), 65
arbitrary/arbitrariness, of relations/ relationships, 4, 8, 16, 19, 21, 48–49, 56, 65
Aristophanes, 28–30, 36
Aristotle, 7, 36–38
    Heidegger, on time, 36n19
    Irigaray, readings on, 7, 22, 25
    "natural difference," 25
    Physics IV, 7, 25, 36–37
    place, on, 7, 38, 38n20, 40–43
    Politics, 26
    Spelman, on 26n2

Babe, 66–67, 98
Bad Faith and Anti-Black Racism (Gordon), 46
Bakare-Yusuf, Bibi, 60
Baker, Houston, 55
Baldwin, James, 79
Beauvoir, Simone de, 12
    Second Sex, The, 21
    sex/gender, on, 21
    transcendence/immanence dichotomy, 12
"belief (liberal) in universal subjectivity," 49
Berg, Alison, 72
Berliner, Alain, 87
    Ma vie en rose (My Life In Pink), 87
Bert and Ernie, 84–89
Bigwood, Carol, 60
binaries/oppositional categories, 5, 12, 33, 35, 37, 40, 55
    dichotomies/dualisms, 4, 11, 14, 27, 36n17, 62
    either . . . or formulations, 5, 8
    form/matter, 42
Birt, Robert, 95, 98
"Black Bodies, White Bodies" (Gilman), 47
"black woman," Jadine Child as, 51–52
Bob (aka Jesus), patient, 65–66
bodies/"the body"
    biological ("natural"), 2–4, 14–15, 18–20, 25, 41, 49, 92, 94
    black/dark, 3–5, 48, 52, 54, 63
    "bleeding"/excess of, 3, 53, 64–65
    body theory/disembodiment of, 3, 59–62

Valerio, Max Wolf, 83, 87, 90, 92–94, 97
violence
 anti-queer/anti-trans, 61, 65, 86, 97.
  See also transgender
Volatile Bodies (Grosz), 33n14

Wallace, Julia, 73–74
Washington, Johnny, 91
Weed, Elizabeth, 74–75
Wendell, Susan, 59
Western philosophy
 blackness within, 47
 dualisms, 4, 11, 11n1, 27. *See also*
  binaries/oppositional categories
 feminine, diverted from, 14
 Irigaray, concern with, 12. *See also*
  Irigaray
 metaphysics/metaphysical, 37–38, 40
 Okin, reflecting on, 26
 opposing binaries, 11, 37, 52, 55
 racism in, 57
 relation between the sexes, 11
 traditional frameworks, 3
 women excluded from, 27, 42

Whitford, Margaret, 33n13
*Why Am I Gay?: Stories of Coming Out
 in America*, 80
"Why is it shocking when a lesbian
 leader falls for a man?"
 (Faderman), 68n7
Wiley Coyote, 67
Winchell, Barry, 86
wombs, 6, 37, 39. *See also* bodies/"the
 body"; containers
women, as objects, 13, 14, 37, 96
women-to-women relations, 23
Woodruff, Paul, 31n7
Wright, Janet, 71–71

Young, Iris Marion, 92

Zeus, 28–30, 36
Zimmerman, Bonnie, 74
Zita, Jacquelyn, 61, 65–66, 89
 "Male Lesbians and the
  Postmodernist Body," 65